# A TREASURY OF VICTORIAN MURDER

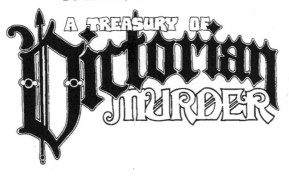

**RICK GEARY** was born in 1946 in Kansas City and grew up in Wichita. After getting a degree in art and film, the West beckoned. San Diego became his new home in 1975. Rick established himself through *Heavy Metal*, *Epic*, the Copley News Service, and especially *National Lampoon* where he cartooned the stranger aspects of The Great American Way of life with his inimitable straight-faced sense of the absurd. This has been collected in his book *Housebound with Rick Geary*. He has also done a lot of whimsical comics and children's comics including for Disney Adventures magazine. He lived in New York City for 4 years where he provided illustrations for the *New York Times* but sunny San Diego proved too hard to stay away from.

# A TREASURY OF VICTORIAN MURDER

Compiled and Illustrated by

RICK GEARY

NBM ComicsLit

ISBN 1-56163-309-7
Library of Congress Control Number: 2002100115
©1987 Rick Geary


5    4    3    2


Comicslit is an imprint and
trademark of

NANTIER · BEALL · MINOUSTCHINE
Publishing inc.
new york

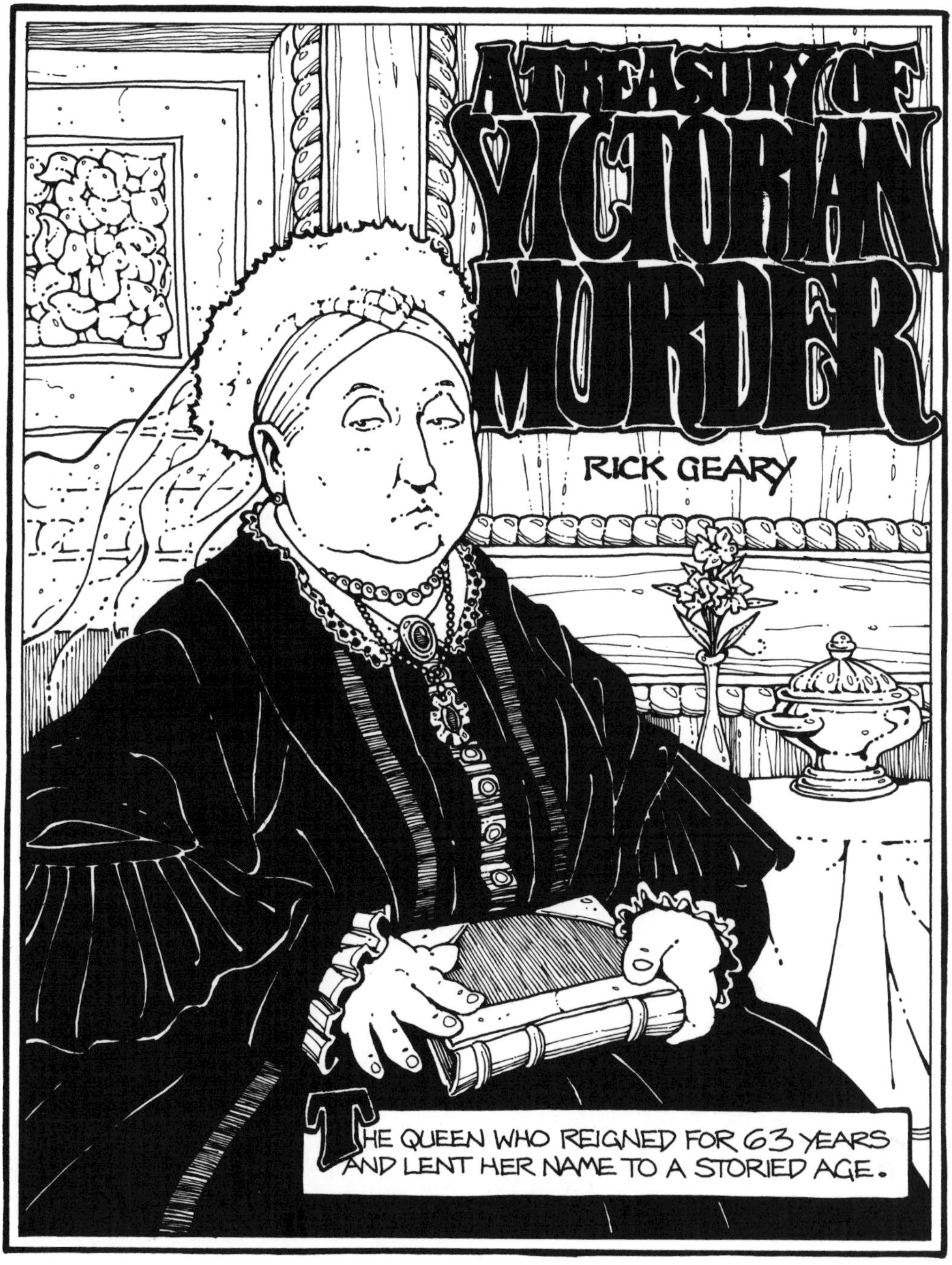
A TREASURY OF
VICTORIAN
MURDER
RICK GEARY
THE QUEEN WHO REIGNED FOR 63 YEARS AND LENT HER NAME TO A STORIED AGE.

Also in the Victorian Murder series:
Jack The Ripper, hc: $15.95, pb.: $7.95
The Borden Tragedy, pb.: $8.95
The Fatal Bullet, pb.: $8.95
The Mystery of Mary Rogers, pb.: $8.95, hc: $15.95

A Treasury of
Victorian Murder
JACK the RIPPER
by
RICK GEARY

We have over 150 titles, write
for our color catalog:
NBM
555 8th Ave., Suite 1202
New York, NY 10018
see our website at
http://www.nbmpublishing.com

A TREASURY OF VICTORIAN MURDER
The Mystery of
Mary Rogers
RICK GEARY

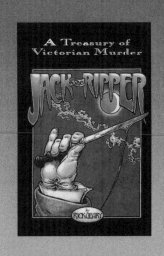

## INTRODUCTORY REMARKS
### and bibliography

The Victorian Age was an especially delectable one for murder. The crimes of that era were characterized not only by the peculiar interpersonal pressures inherent in a rapidly industrializing, sexually repressive society, but by the energy and attentiveness of the popular press, then in the first blush of its sensationalistic power. No detail was too insignificant, no rumor too outlandish to see print in those rambunctious times. The big city dailies were just coming into their own as molders of mass opinion, and all of the cases presented here were followed and speculated upon by an insatiable public.

The Dr. Pritchard case, the longest in the book, was detailed daily in the spring of 1865 by The Glasgow Herald, The Scotsman, and The Courant. It was retold around the turn of the century by the Scot William Roughead, murder buff supreme and one of the first serious compilers of true crime stories (reprinted in the 1951 collection *Classic Crimes*). The case was again related by Jack House, a Roughead protegee, in his 1961 book *Square Mile of Murder*, a study of four famous Glasgow murders of the Victorian Age.

The Ryan tragedy of 1873 was and remains one of the most puzzling of New York's early unsolved murders. It was reported, with all the information then available, by Inspector Thomas Byrnes, the city's formidable Chief of Detectives, in his 1886 *Encyclopedia of Professional Criminals of America.*

The final case presented here, that of Mrs. Pearcey, excited headlines throughout England in 1890. Its only retelling, brief and tantalizing, was by the British crime historians J.H.H. Gaute and Robin Odell in their comprehensive *The Murderers' Who's Who*, first published in 1979.

Rick Geary
San Diego, 1987

Dedicated to my wife Deborah

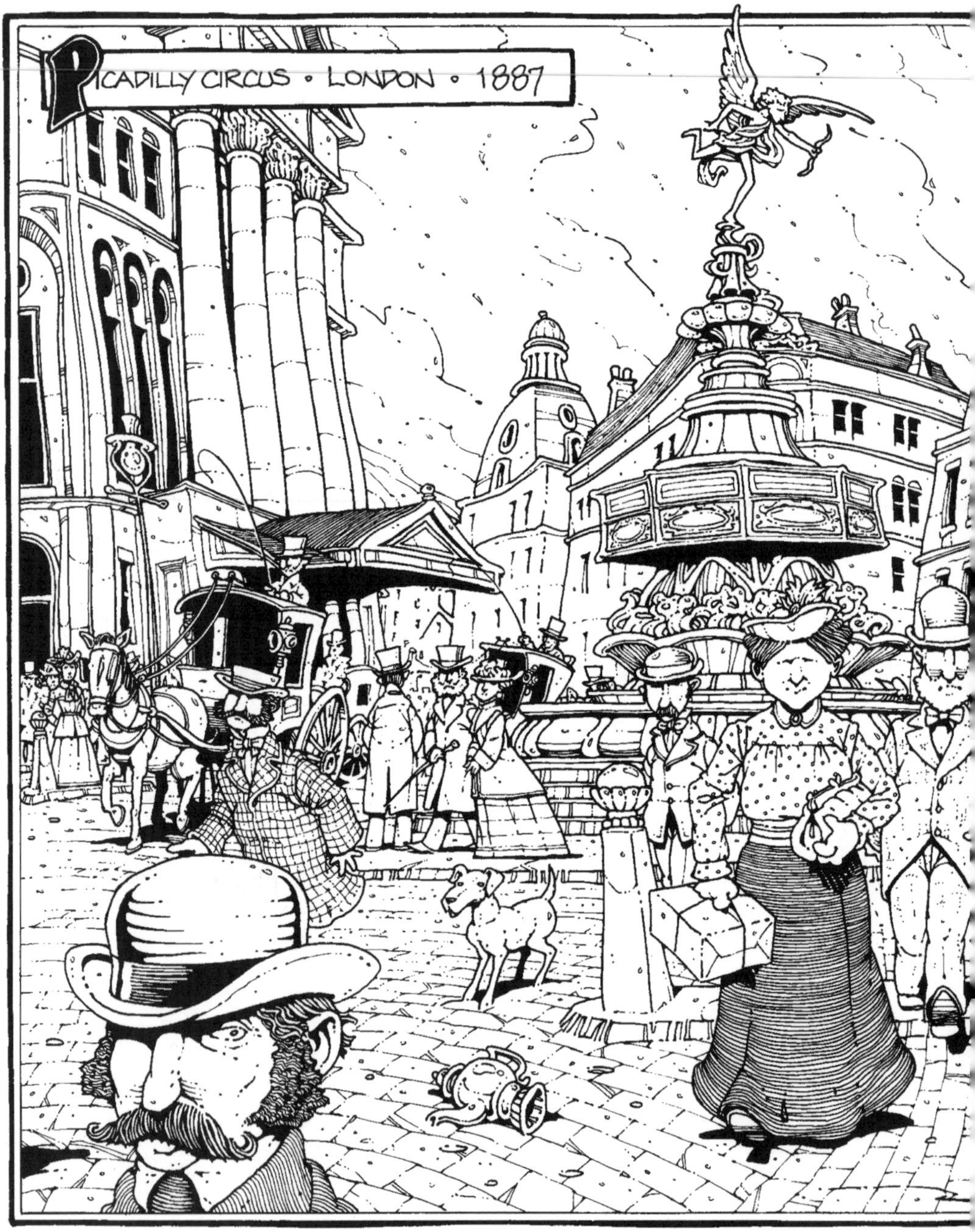
PICADILLY CIRCUS • LONDON • 1887

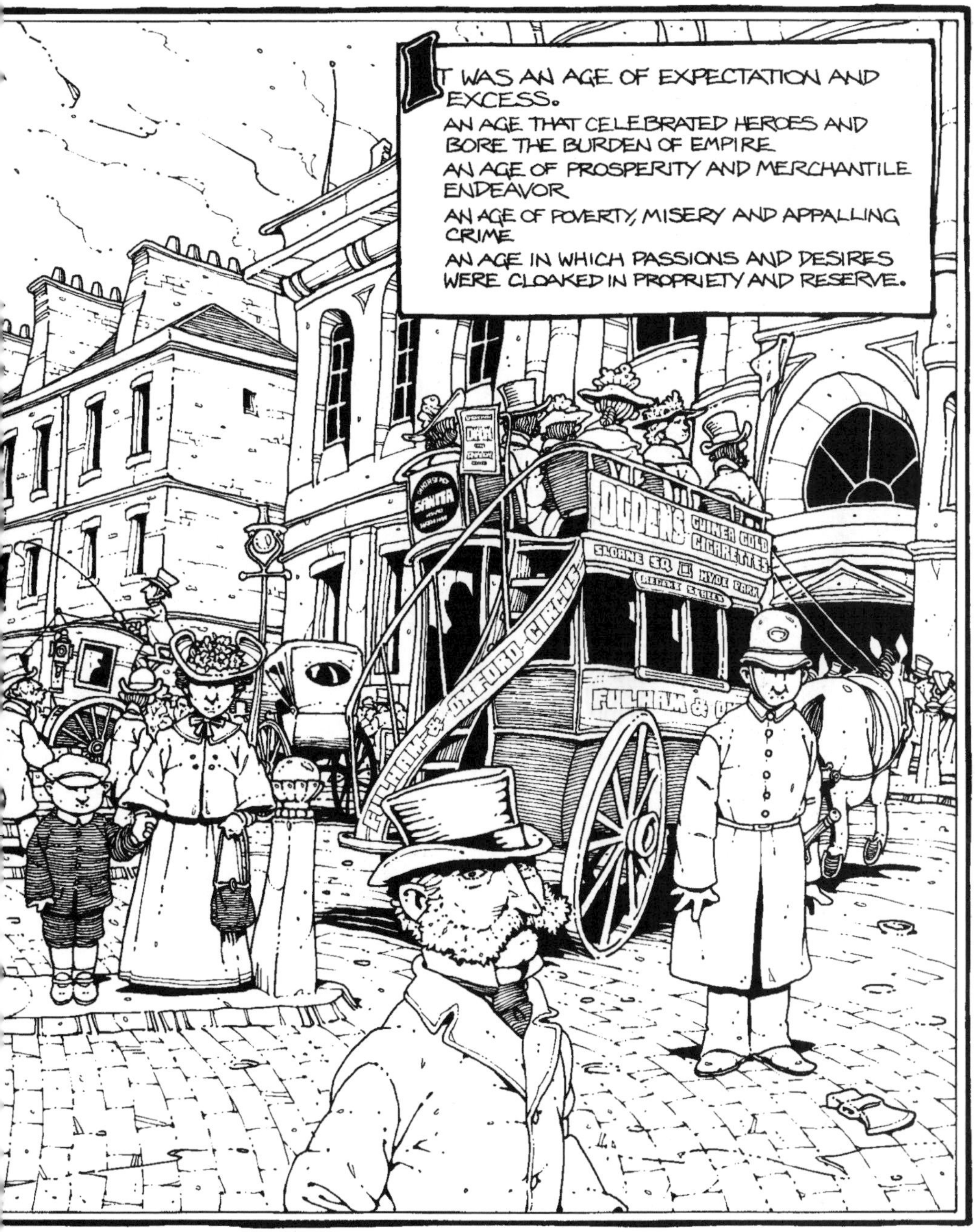
IT WAS AN AGE OF EXPECTATION AND EXCESS.
AN AGE THAT CELEBRATED HEROES AND BORE THE BURDEN OF EMPIRE
AN AGE OF PROSPERITY AND MERCHANTILE ENDEAVOR
AN AGE OF POVERTY, MISERY AND APPALLING CRIME
AN AGE IN WHICH PASSIONS AND DESIRES WERE CLOAKED IN PROPRIETY AND RESERVE.
OGDEN'S GUINEA GOLD CIGARETTES
SLOANE SQ. HYDE PARK
FULHAM & OXFORD CIRCUS
FULHAM & O

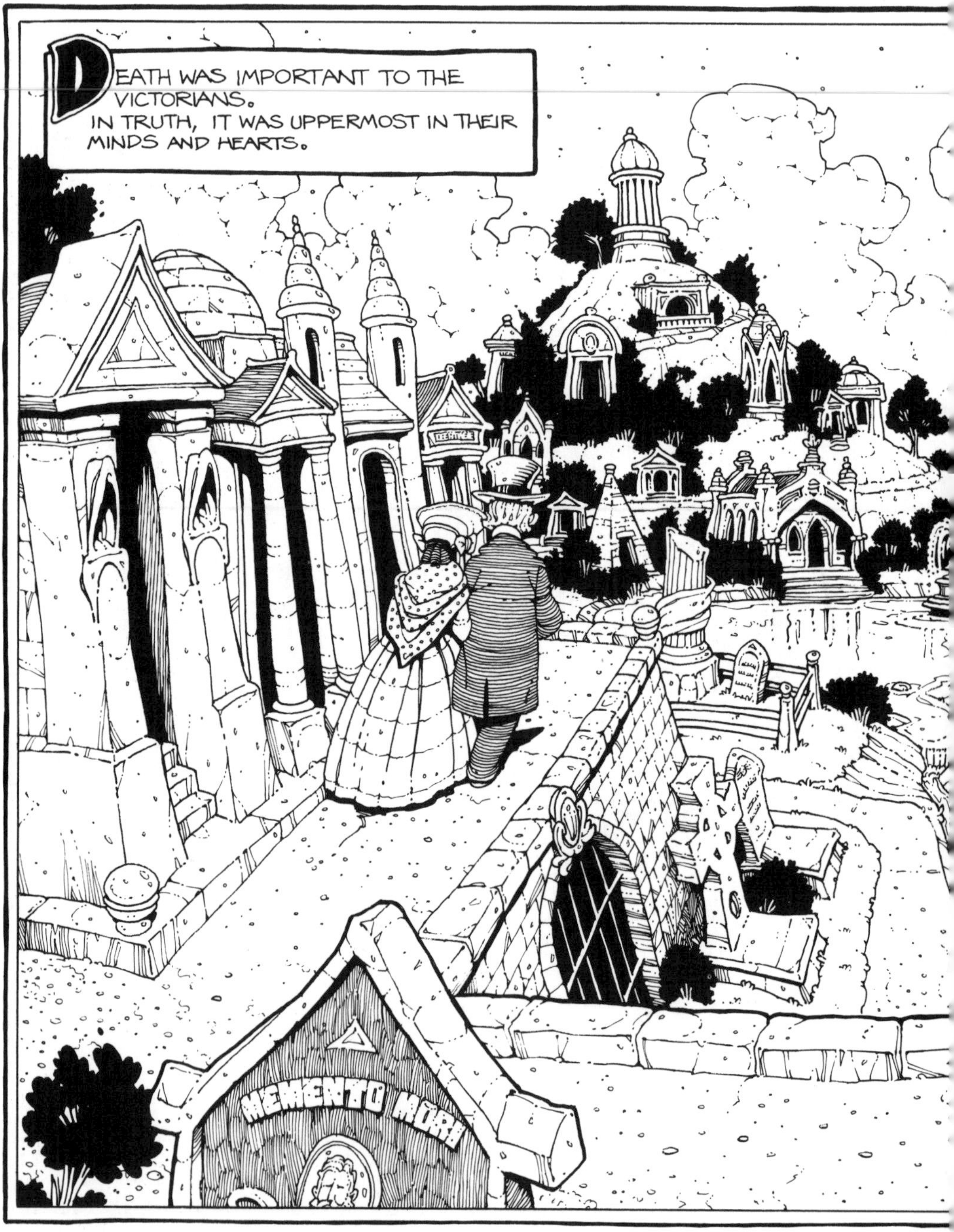
DEATH WAS IMPORTANT TO THE VICTORIANS.
IN TRUTH, IT WAS UPPERMOST IN THEIR MINDS AND HEARTS.
MEMENTO MORI

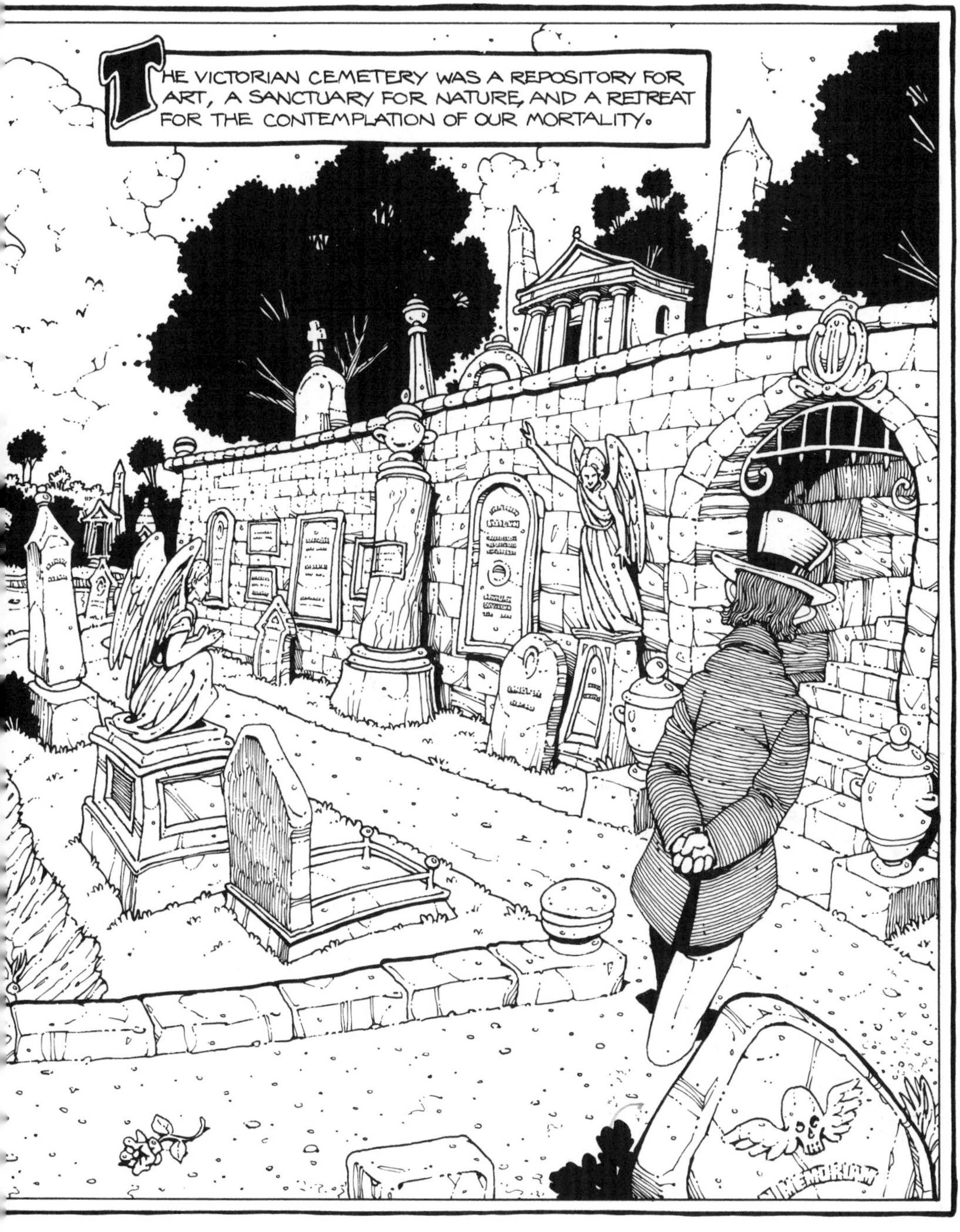
THE VICTORIAN CEMETERY WAS A REPOSITORY FOR ART, A SANCTUARY FOR NATURE, AND A RETREAT FOR THE CONTEMPLATION OF OUR MORTALITY.
IN MEMORIAM

# CELEBRATED EVENTS OF THE VICTORIAN AGE

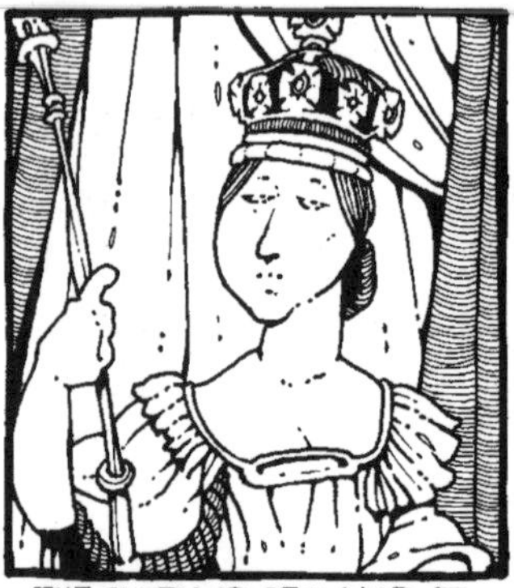

THE QUEEN IS CROWNED AT WESTMINSTER ABBEY (28 JAN 1838)

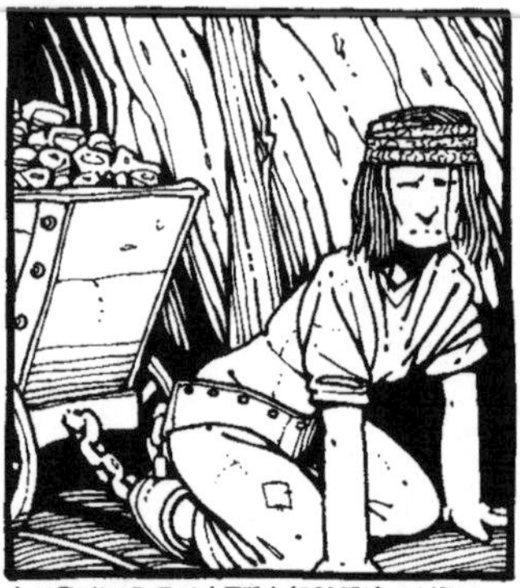

WORKING DAY OF WOMEN AND CHILDREN REDUCED TO 10 HRS (1847)

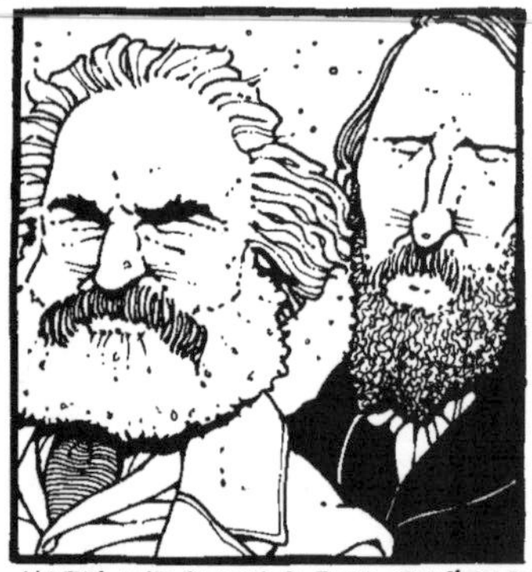

MARX AND ENGELS PUBLISH "THE COMMUNIST MANIFESTO" (1848)

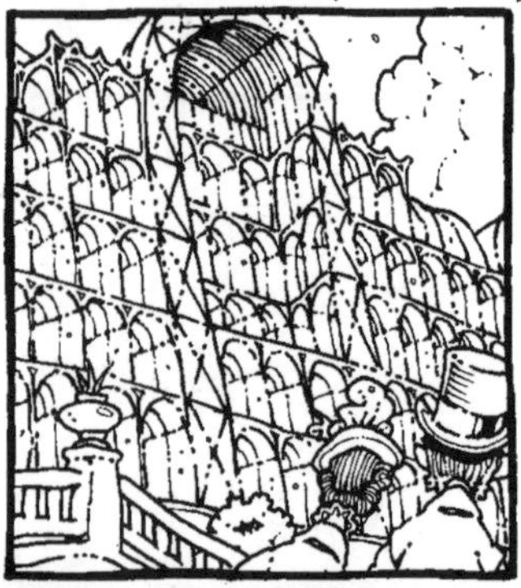

THE GREAT EXHIBITION DISPLAYS BRITISH WARES TO THE WORLD (1851)

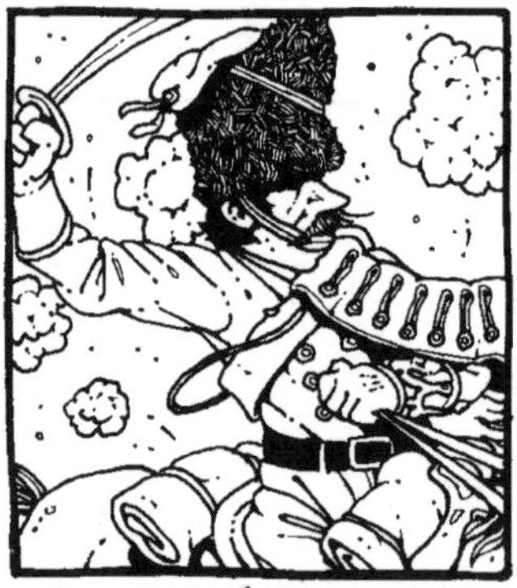

THE ILL-FATED "CHARGE OF THE LIGHT BRIGADE" (18 OCT 1854)

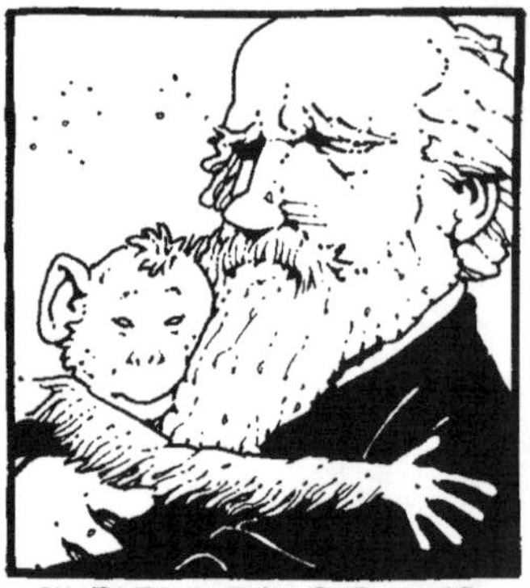

CHARLES DARWIN PUBLISHES "THE ORIGIN OF SPECIES" (1859)

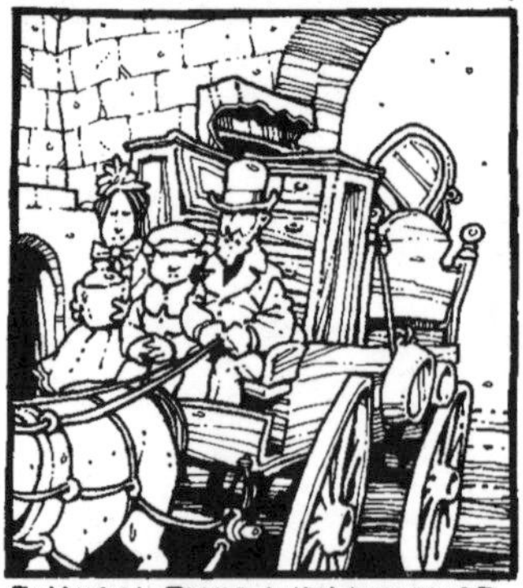

FINANCIAL PANIC AND WORLDWIDE DEPRESSION (1873)

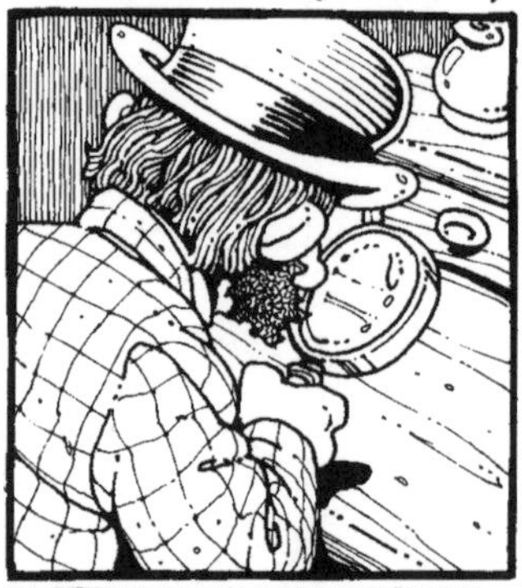

FINGERPRINT EXAMINATION FIRST USED IN CRIMINAL INQUIRY (1885)

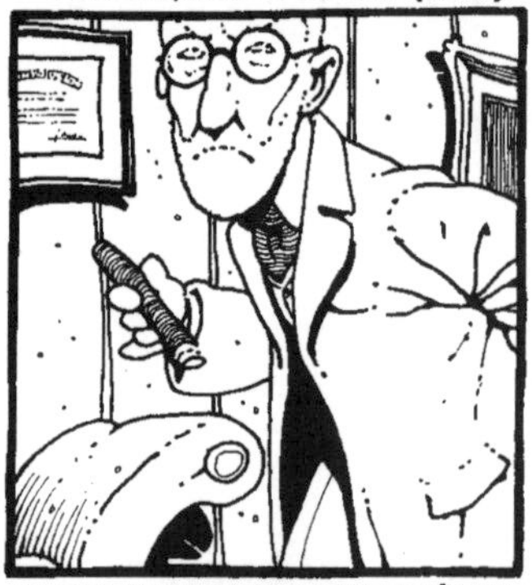

SIGMUND FREUD PUBLISHES "THE INTERPRETATION OF DREAMS" (1900)

# ILLUSTRIOUS PERSONAGES
## OF THE VICTORIAN AGE

### STATESMEN, EXPLORERS, INNOVATORS

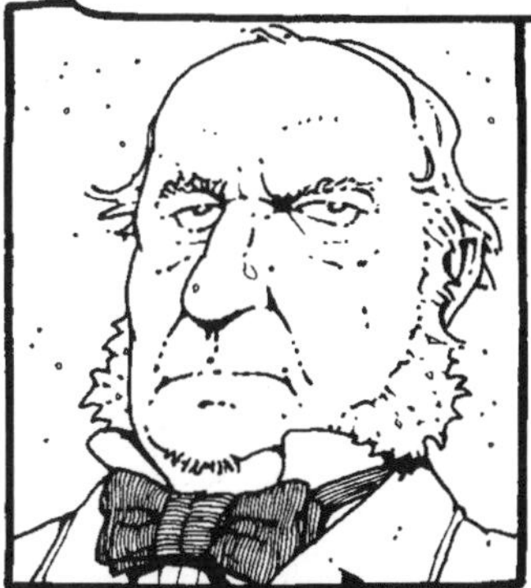

WILLIAM E. GLADSTONE: FOUR TIMES PRIME MINISTER

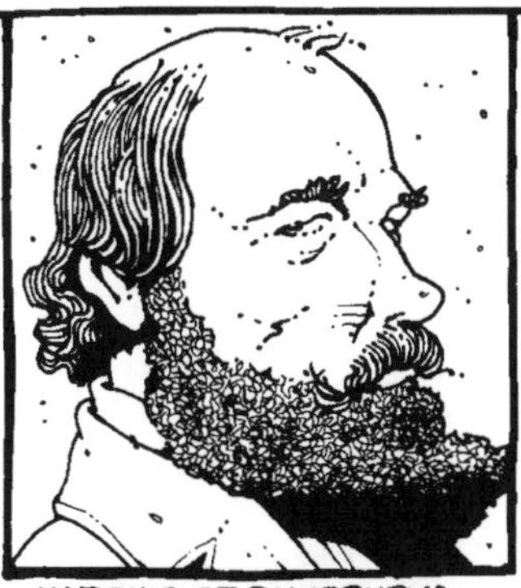

MARQUIS OF SALISBURY: STATESMAN AND INTELLECTUAL

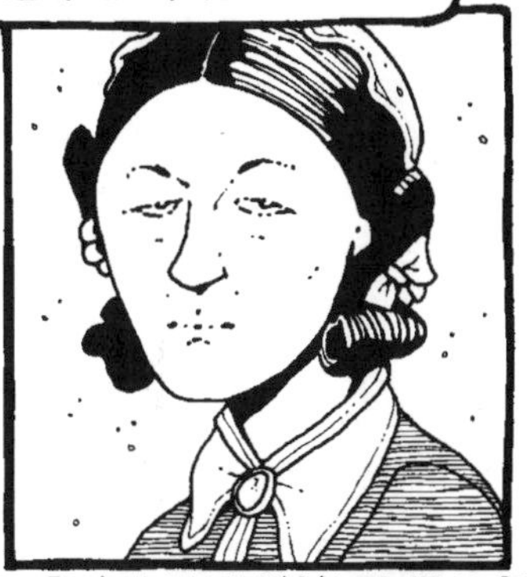

FLORENCE NIGHTINGALE: VALIANT NURSE, HEROINE OF THE CRIMEA

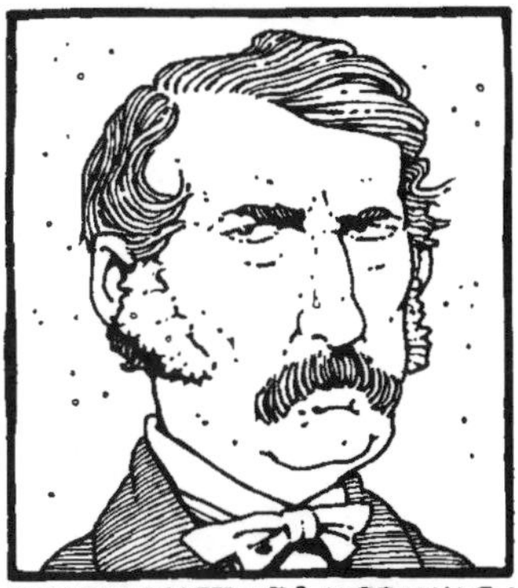

DAVID LIVINGSTONE: MISSIONARY, EXPLORER, CRUSADER AGAINST SLAVERY

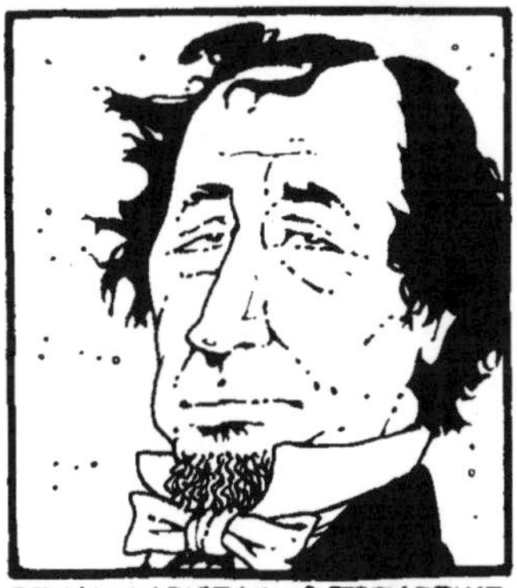

BENJAMIN DISRAELI: TORY PRIME MINISTER, THE QUEEN'S FAVORITE

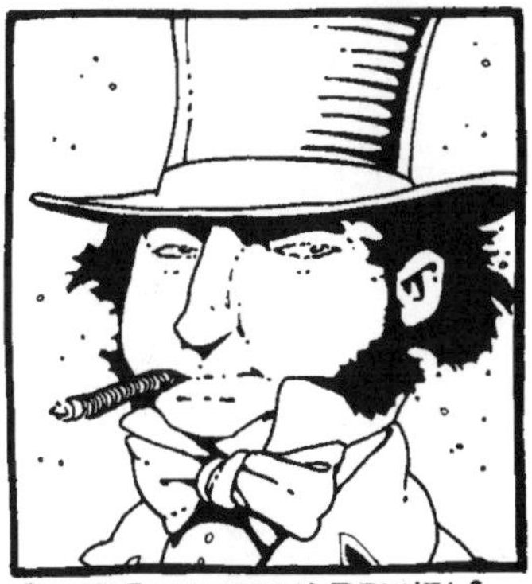

ISAMBARD KINGDOM BRUNEL: FLAMBOYANT ENGINEERING GENIUS

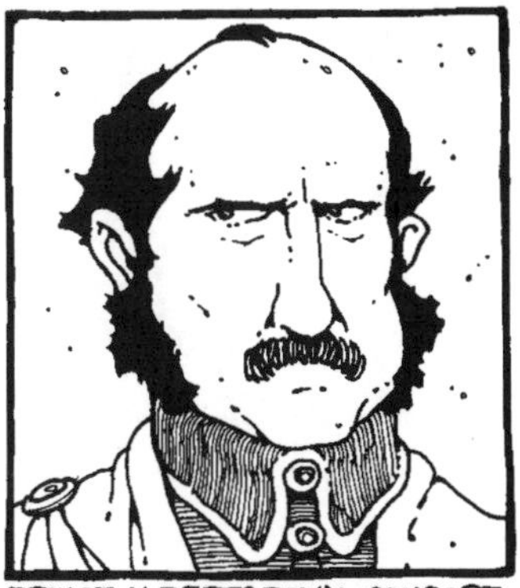

PRINCE ALBERT: ROYAL CONSORT, PROMOTER OF BRITISH COMMERCE

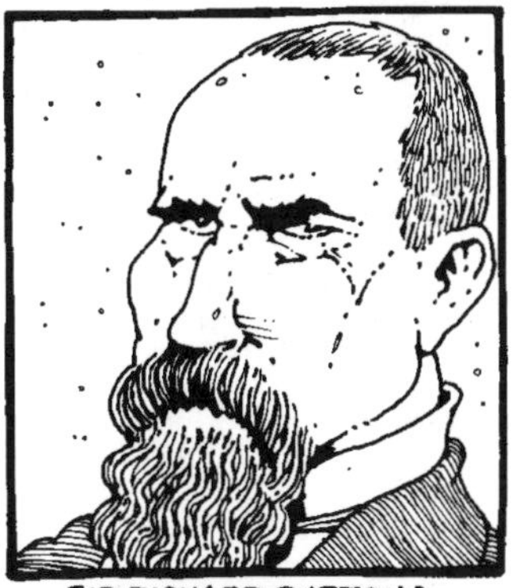

SIR RICHARD BURTON: DIPLOMAT AND ADVENTURER

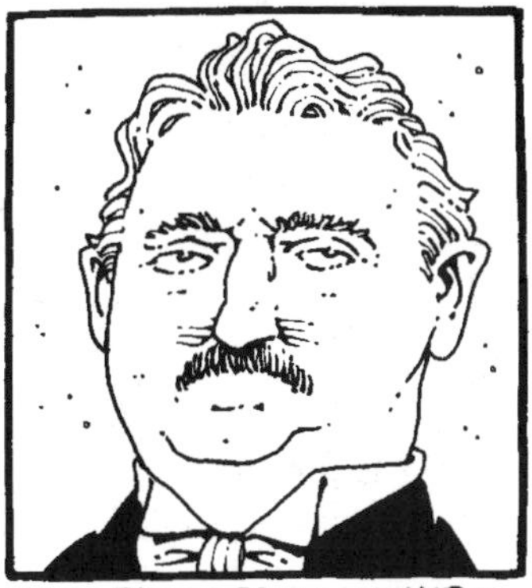

CECIL RHODES: MILLIONAIRE, EMPIRE BUILDER

# LITERATURE AND THE ARTS

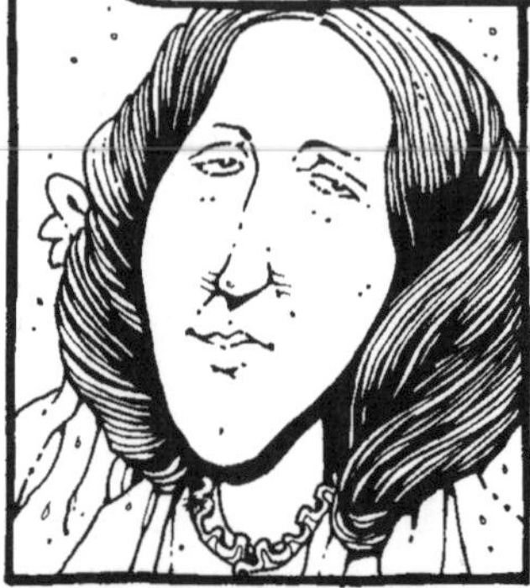

GEORGE ELIOT (MARYANN EVANS) WROTE NOVELS RICH IN CHARACTER

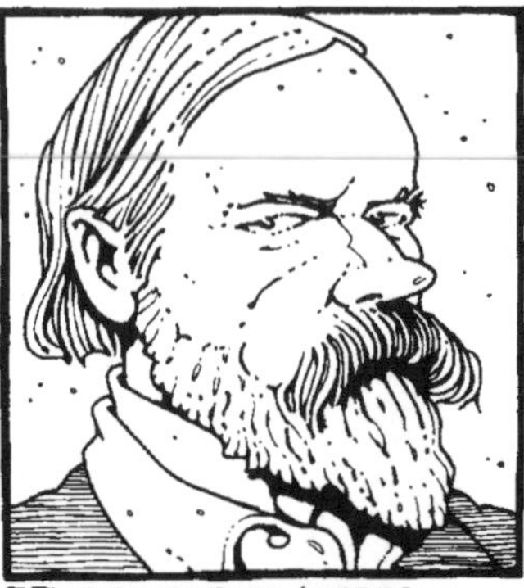

EDWARD BURNE-JONES: PAINTER OF MYTH AND ALLEGORY

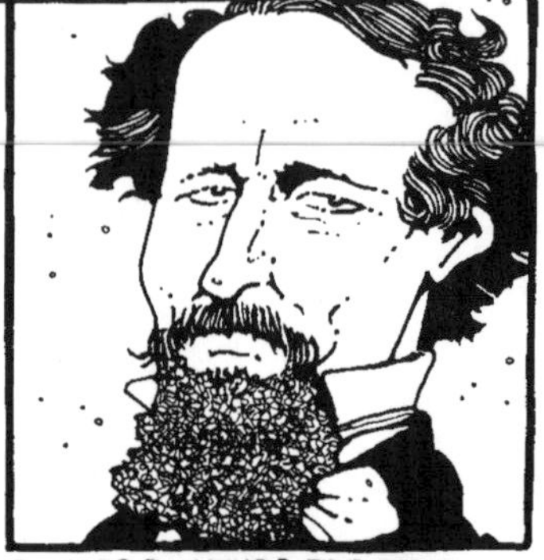

CHARLES DICKENS: PRE-EMINENT NOVELIST, SOCIAL CRUSADER

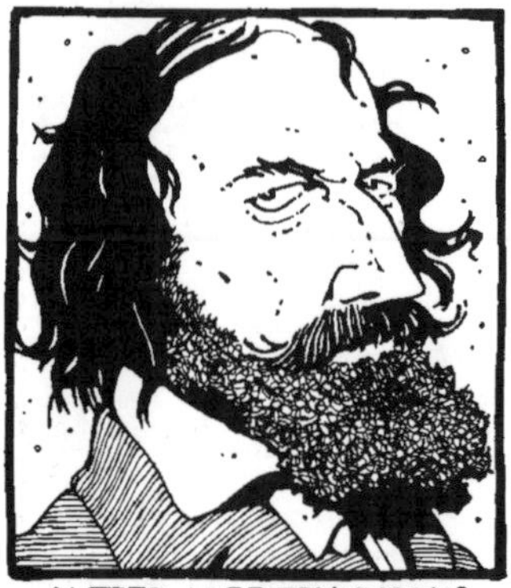

ALFRED, LORD TENNYSON: POET LAUREATE

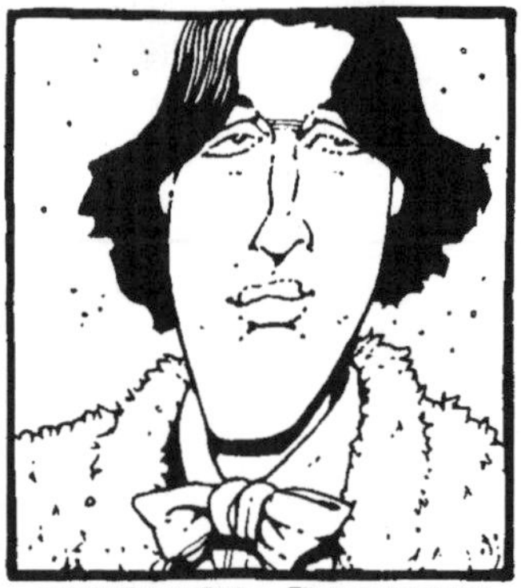

OSCAR WILDE: PLAYWRIGHT AND WIT EXTRAORDINAIRE

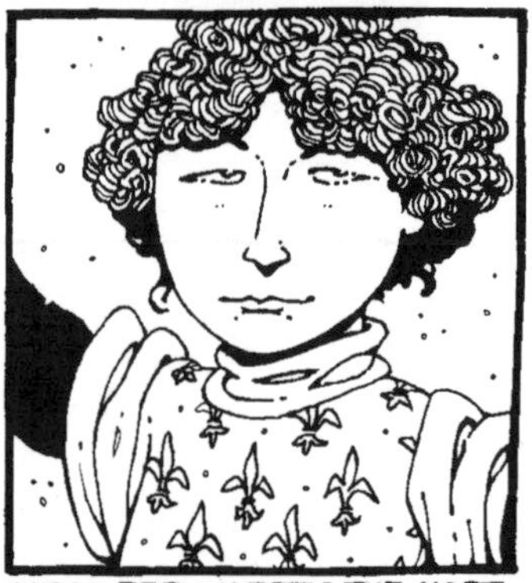

SARAH BERNHARDT: THE MOST CELEBRATED ACTRESS OF THE AGE

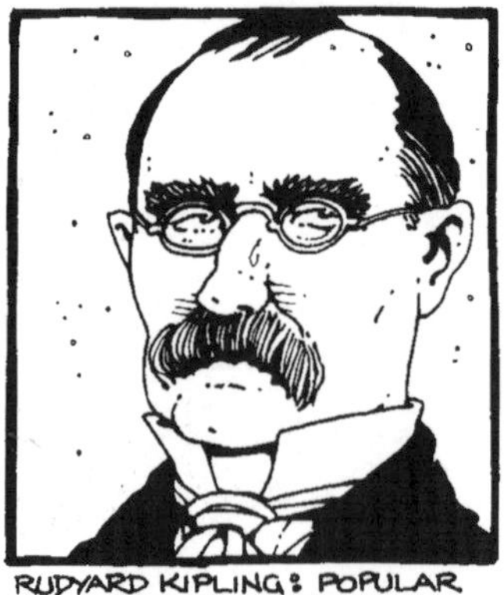

RUDYARD KIPLING: POPULAR POET OF EMPIRE.

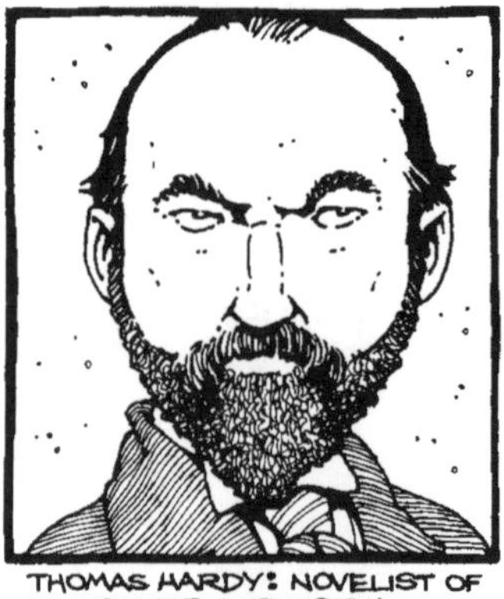

THOMAS HARDY: NOVELIST OF POWER AND VISION

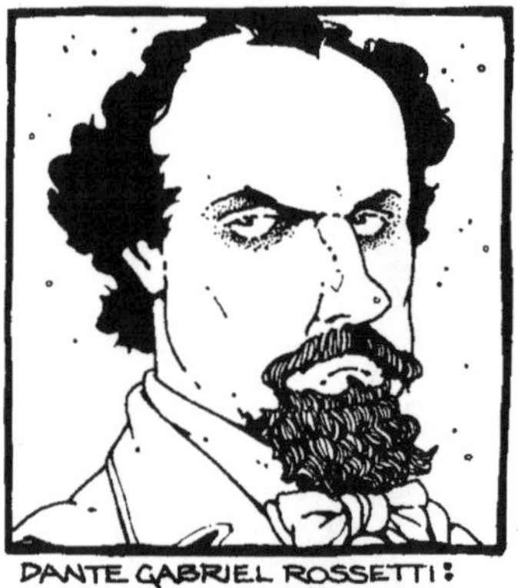

DANTE GABRIEL ROSSETTI: TORMENTED PAINTER AND POET

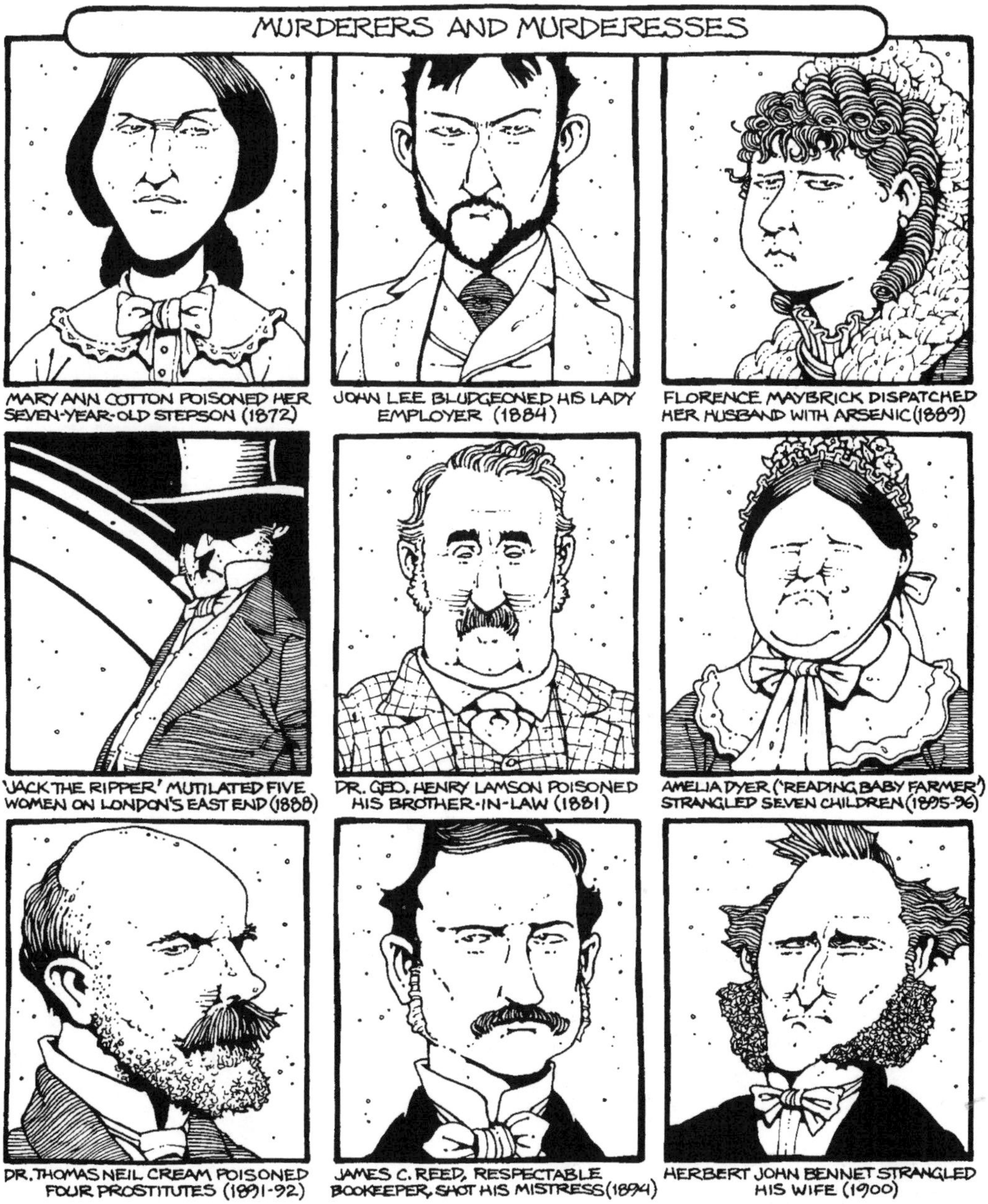
MURDERERS AND MURDERESSES
MARY ANN COTTON POISONED HER SEVEN-YEAR-OLD STEPSON (1872)
JOHN LEE BLUDGEONED HIS LADY EMPLOYER (1884)
FLORENCE MAYBRICK DISPATCHED HER HUSBAND WITH ARSENIC (1889)
'JACK THE RIPPER' MUTILATED FIVE WOMEN ON LONDON'S EAST END (1888)
DR. GEO. HENRY LAMSON POISONED HIS BROTHER-IN-LAW (1881)
AMELIA DYER ('READING BABY FARMER') STRANGLED SEVEN CHILDREN (1895-96)
DR. THOMAS NEIL CREAM POISONED FOUR PROSTITUTES (1891-92)
JAMES C. REED, RESPECTABLE BOOKEEPER, SHOT HIS MISTRESS (1894)
HERBERT JOHN BENNET STRANGLED HIS WIFE (1900)

# MURDERERS AND MURDERESSES

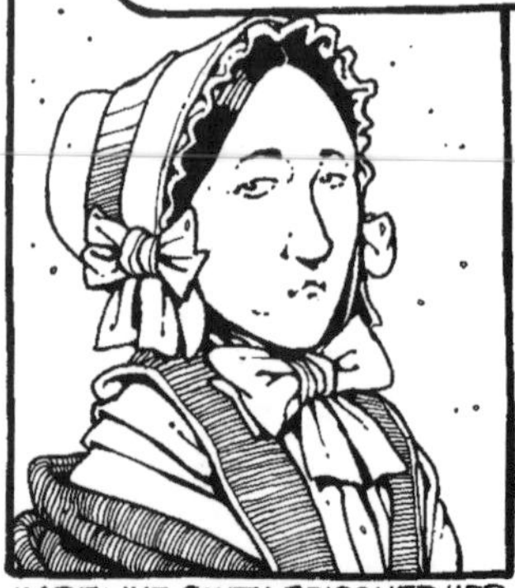

MADELINE SMITH POISONED HER DISCARDED LOVER (1857)

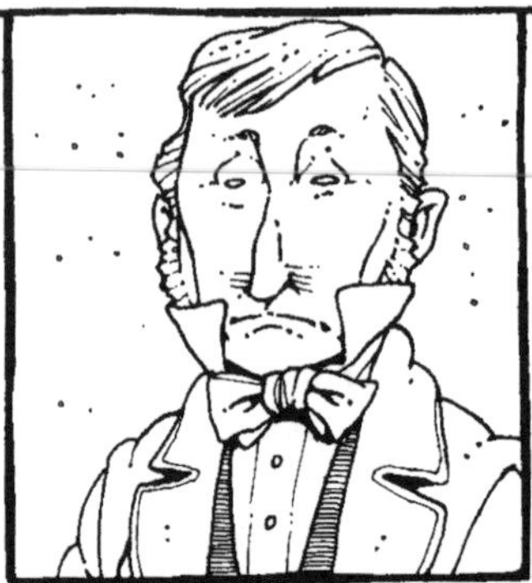

JAMES B. RUSH ('KILLER IN THE FOG') SHOT HIS EMPLOYER AND SON (1848)

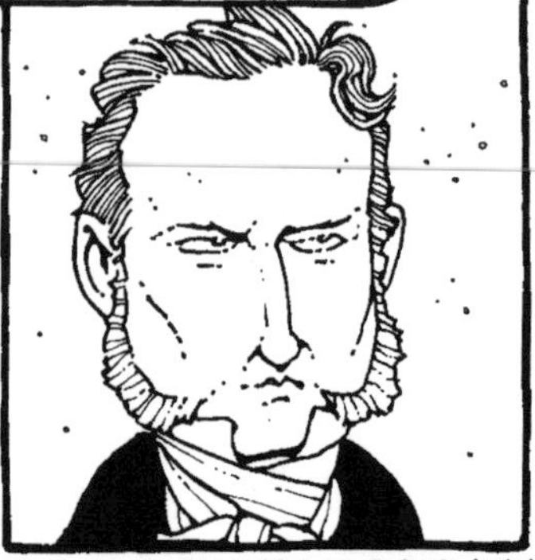

DR. WILLIAM PALMER: POISONED JOHN COOK AND POSSIBLY 14 OTHERS (1855)

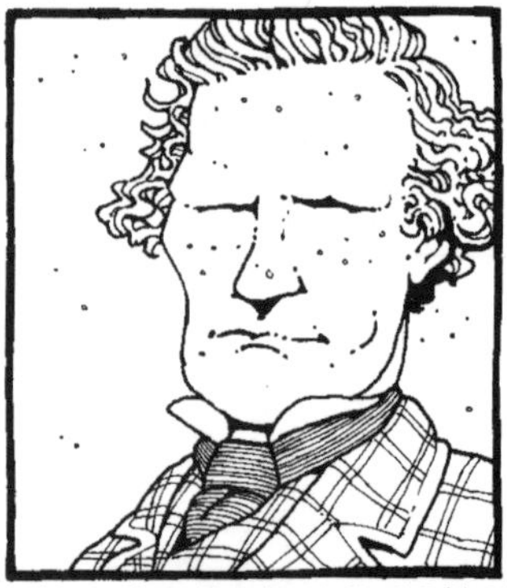

FRANZ MULLER BLUDGEONED THOS. BRIGGS IN FIRST RAILWAY MURDER (1864)

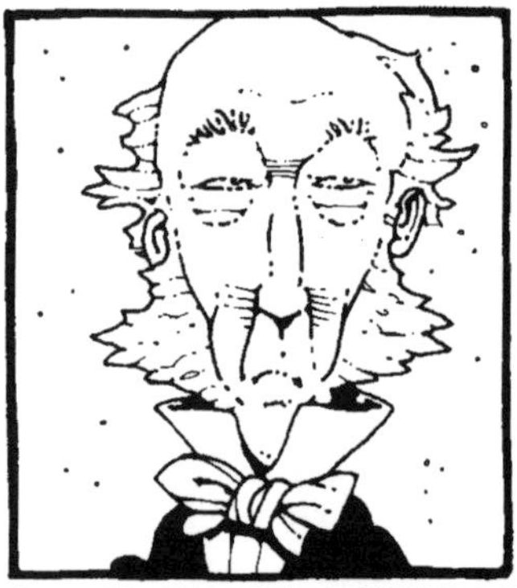

JOHN SELBY WATSON, CLERIC AND SCHOLAR, BLUDGEONED HIS WIFE (1871)

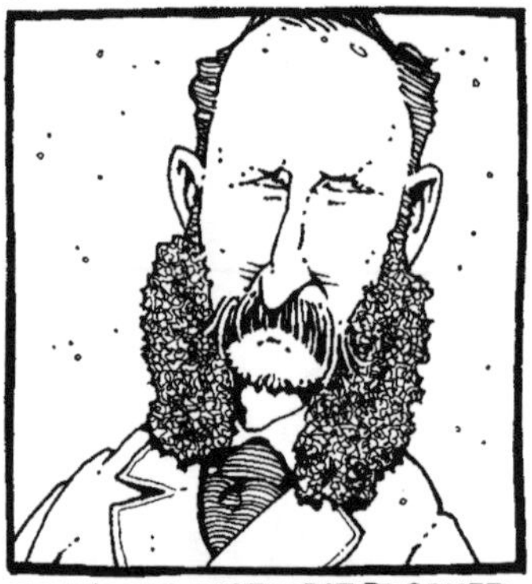

DR. THOMAS SMETHURST POISONED HIS WIFE ISABELLA (1859)

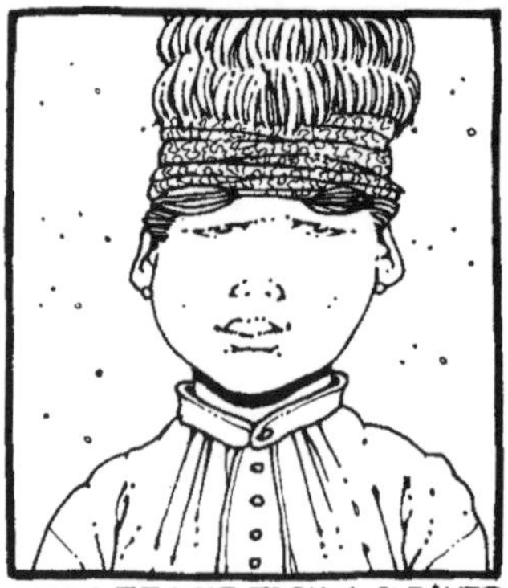

KATE WEBSTER TOOK A CLEAVER TO HER EMPLOYER MRS. THOMAS (1879)

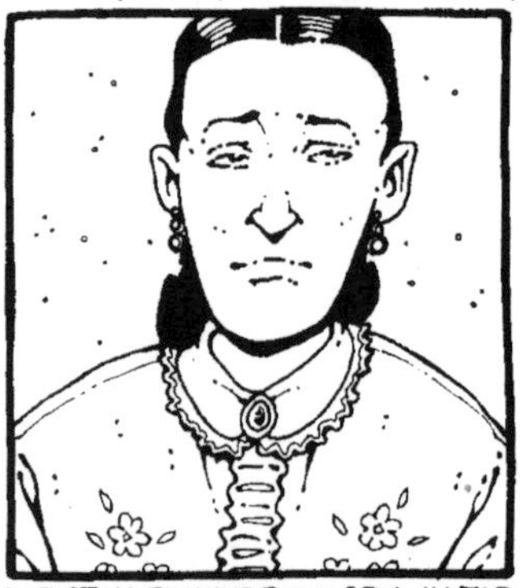

CHRISTINA EDMUNDS KILLED A 4-YEAR-OLD BOY WITH POISONED CHOCOLATES (1871)

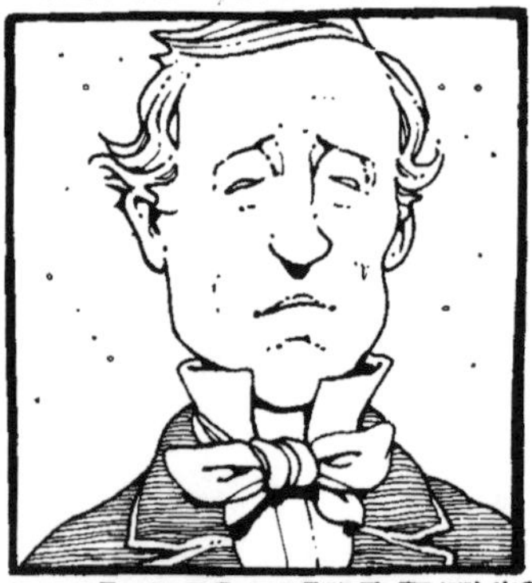

SIMON FRASER BATTERED TO DEATH HIS YOUNG SON "THROUGH MY SLEEP" (1878)

# THE RYAN MYSTERY

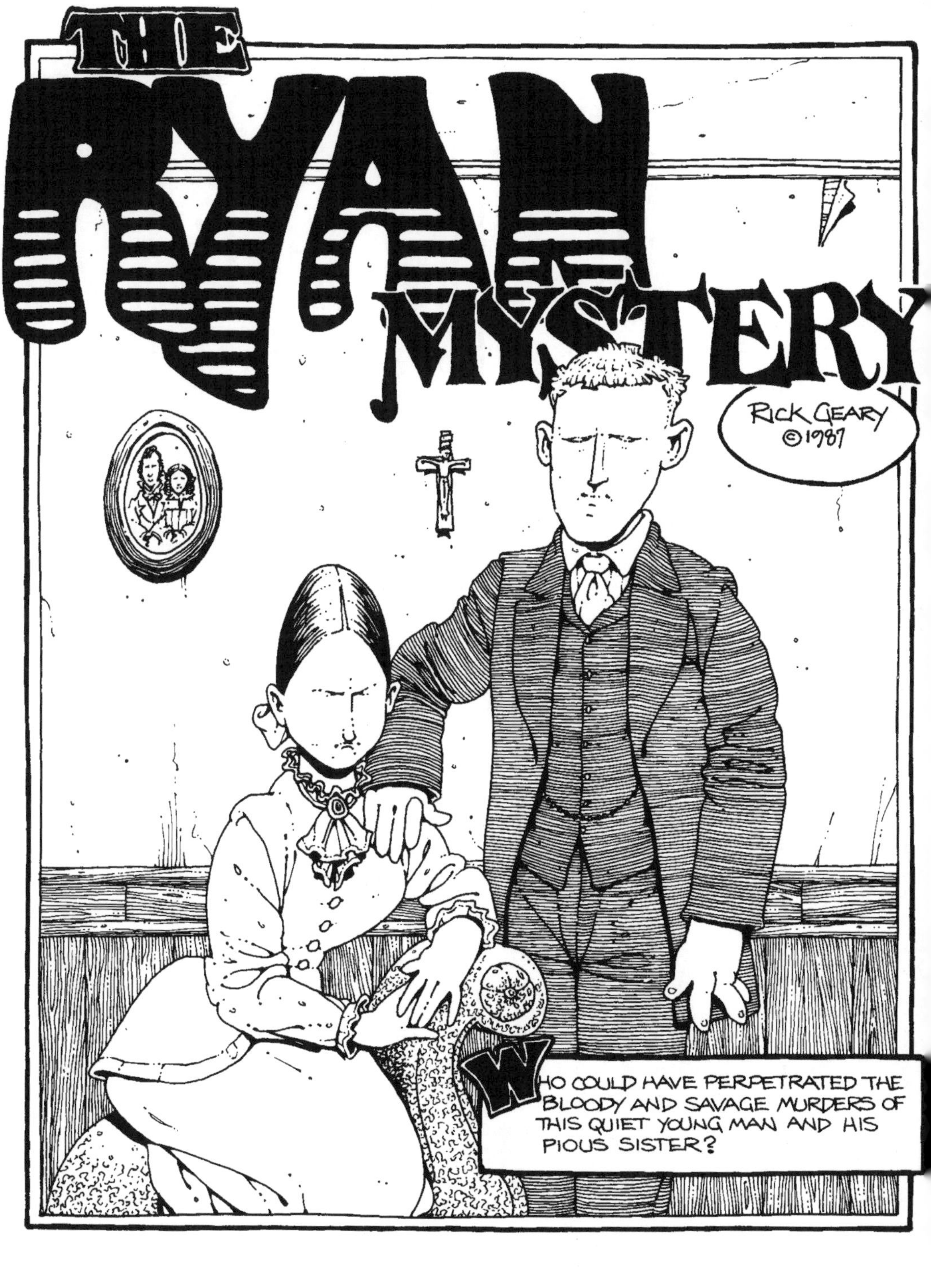
THE
RYAN MYSTERY
RICK GEARY ©1987
WHO COULD HAVE PERPETRATED THE BLOODY AND SAVAGE MURDERS OF THIS QUIET YOUNG MAN AND HIS PIOUS SISTER?

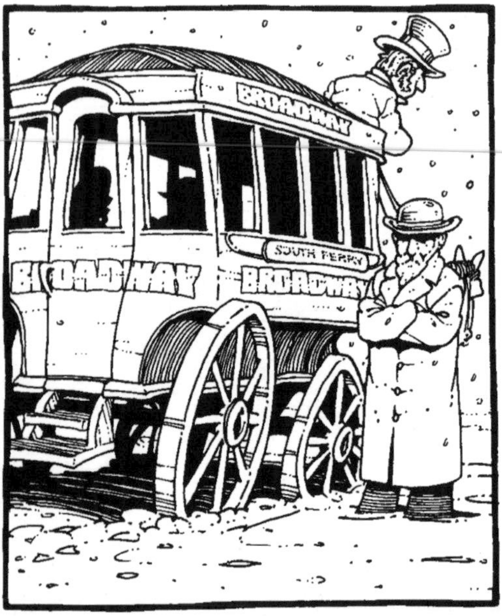
BROADWAY
SOUTH FERRY
BROADWAY
BROADWAY

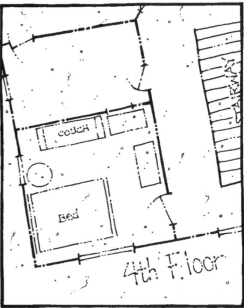

THE CITY OF NEW YORK IN THE WINTER OF 1873

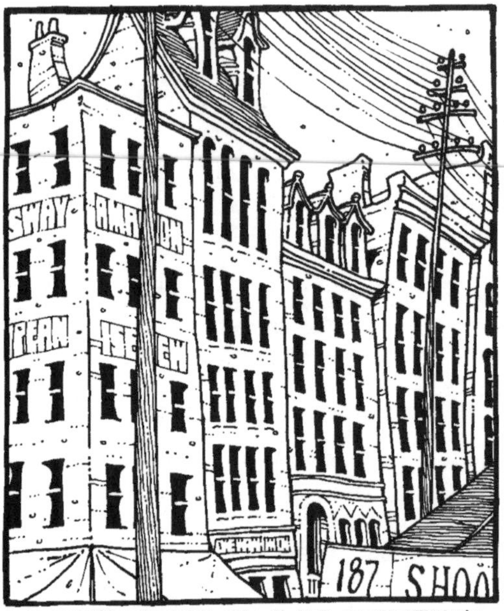
187

THE QUIET AVENUES OF LOWER MANHATTAN: AN UNLIKELY SETTING, ONE WOULD THINK, FOR SUCH A HEINOUS EVENT.

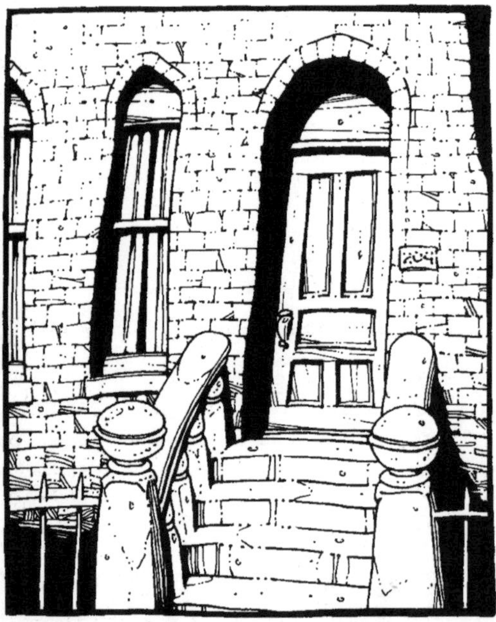
204

NICHOLAS AND MARY RYAN, UNMARRIED BROTHER AND SISTER, LIVED IN THIS TENEMENT AT 204 BROOME STREET.

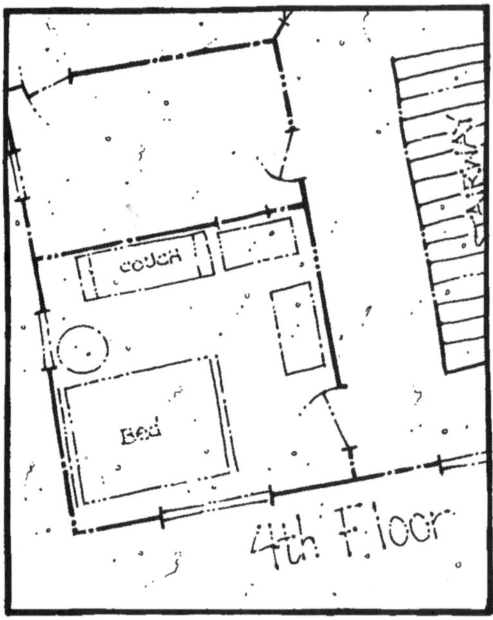
COUCH
Bed
STAIRWAY
4th Floor

THEY OCCUPIED A FRONT ROOM OF THE FOURTH FLOOR.

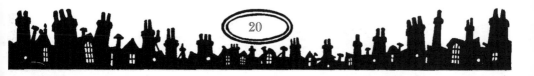

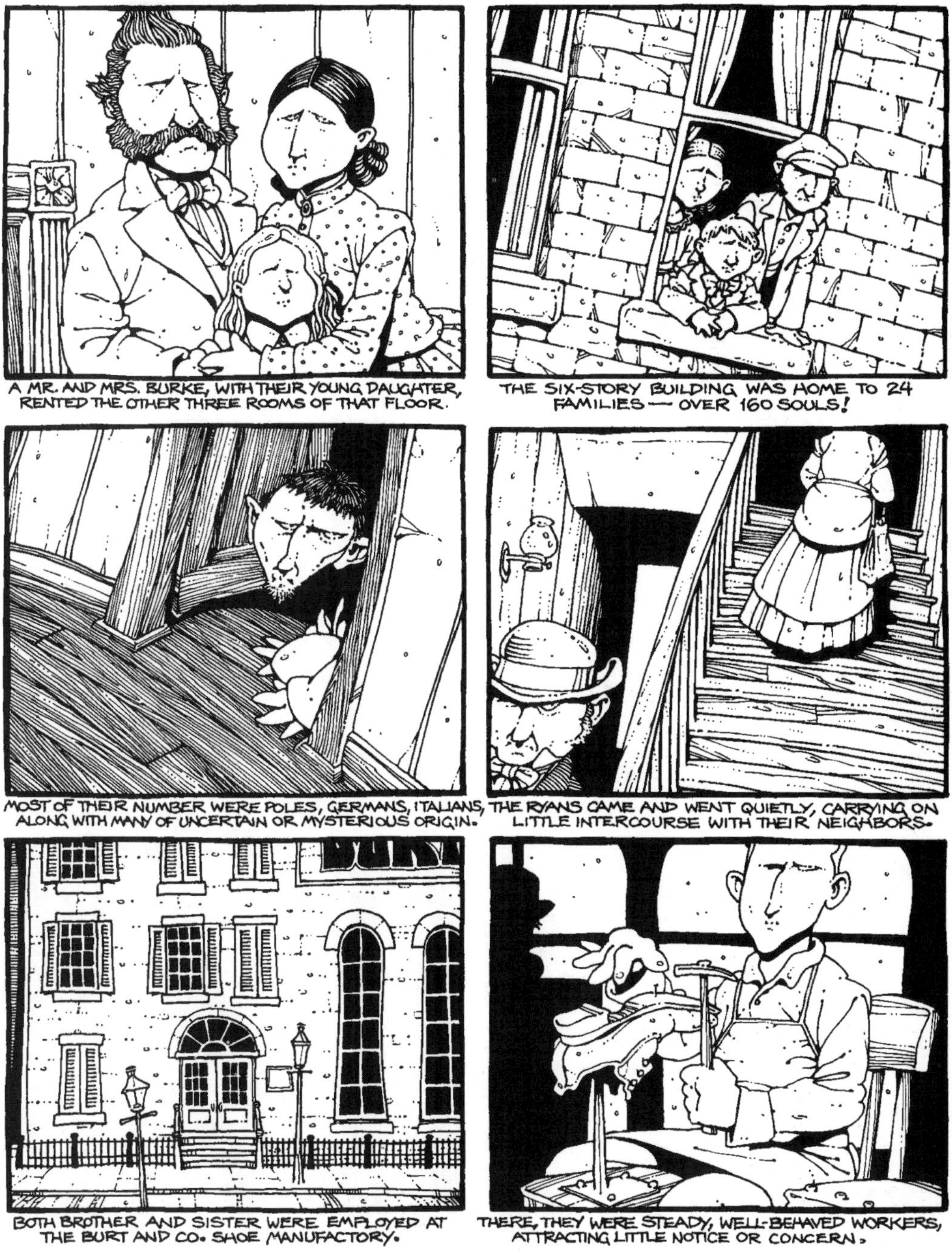
A MR. AND MRS. BURKE, WITH THEIR YOUNG DAUGHTER, RENTED THE OTHER THREE ROOMS OF THAT FLOOR.
THE SIX-STORY BUILDING WAS HOME TO 24 FAMILIES — OVER 160 SOULS!
MOST OF THEIR NUMBER WERE POLES, GERMANS, ITALIANS, ALONG WITH MANY OF UNCERTAIN OR MYSTERIOUS ORIGIN.
THE RYANS CAME AND WENT QUIETLY, CARRYING ON LITTLE INTERCOURSE WITH THEIR NEIGHBORS.
BOTH BROTHER AND SISTER WERE EMPLOYED AT THE BURT AND CO. SHOE MANUFACTORY.
THERE, THEY WERE STEADY, WELL-BEHAVED WORKERS, ATTRACTING LITTLE NOTICE OR CONCERN.

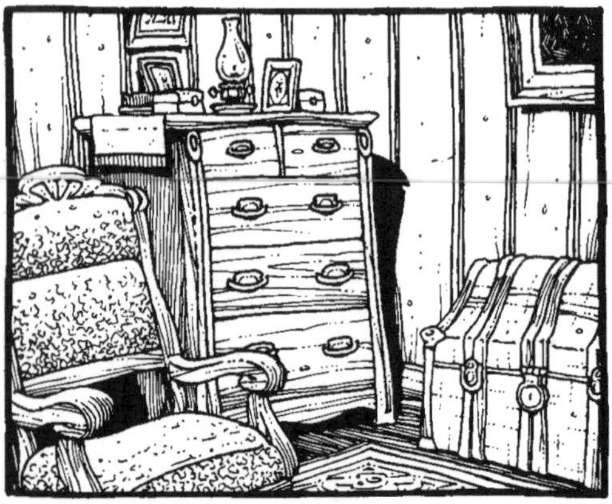

THEIR ROOM WAS SMALL BUT COMFORTABLY FURNISHED

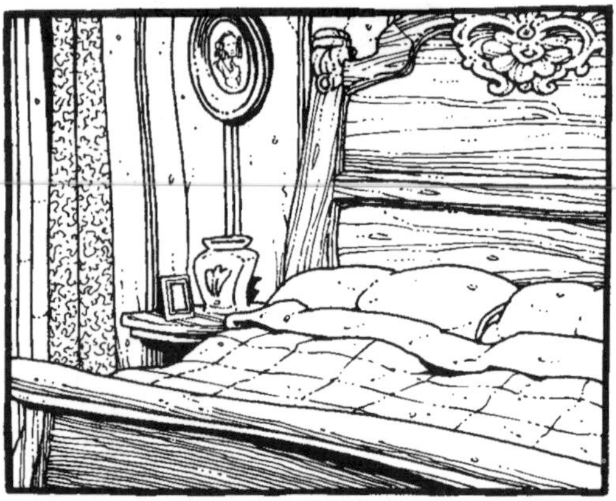

APPARENTLY NICHOLAS RYAN OCCUPIED THE PLUSH, SPACIOUS BED.

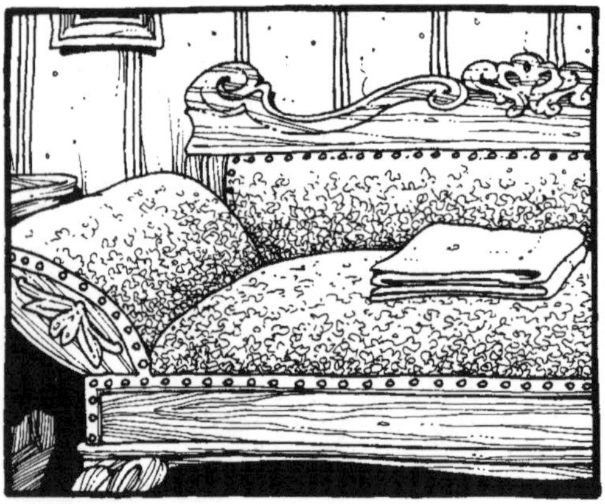

WHILE MARY RYAN SLEPT UPON THE COARSE HORSEHAIR SOFA.

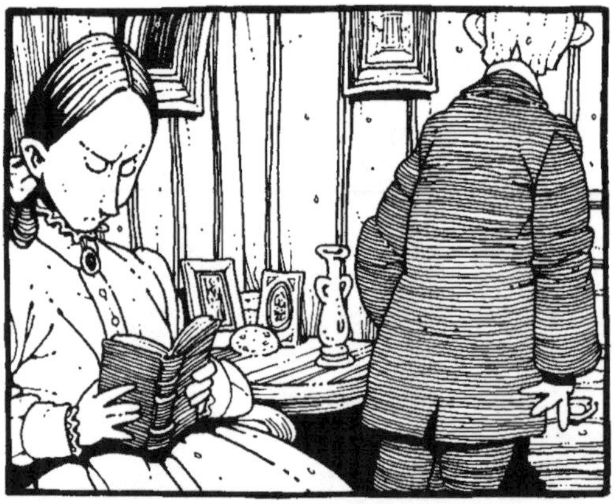

BOTH HAD TEMPERAMENTS MELANCHOLIC, DARK AND DISTANT.

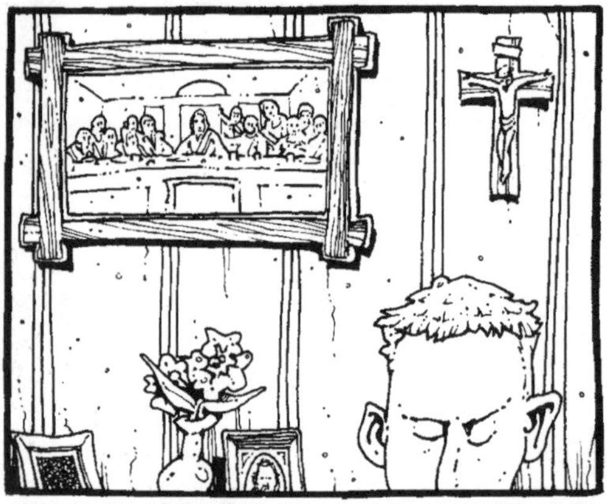

YET THEY APPEARED TO LIVE CONTENTEDLY IN THAT ROOM, RARELY GOING OUT OF AN EVENING.

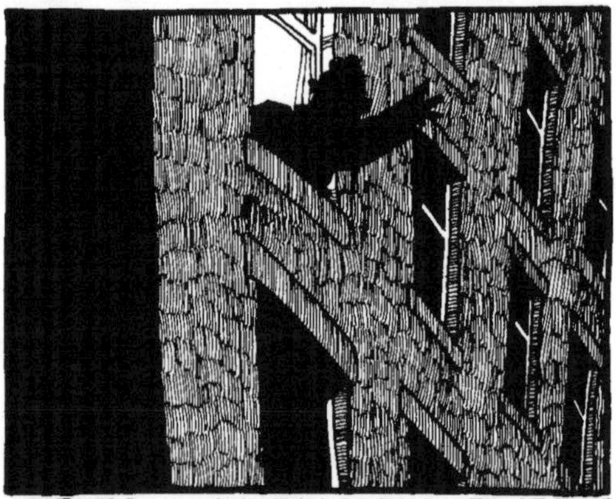

AT ABOUT 3 A.M. ON MONDAY, 22 DECEMBER, CRIES OF "MURDER" ISSUED FROM THE FOURTH FLOOR WINDOW OF 204 BROOME ST.

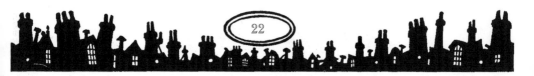

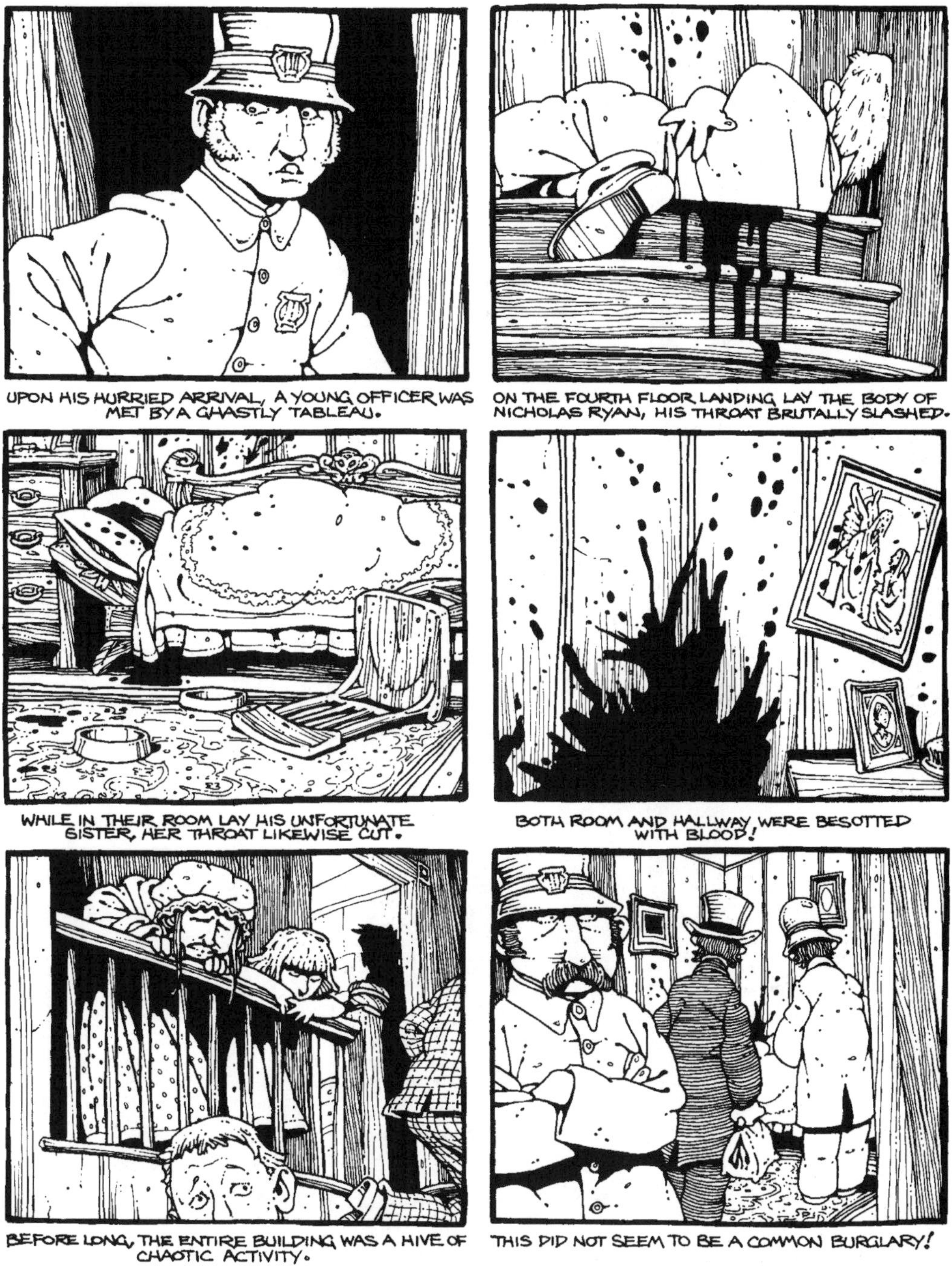
UPON HIS HURRIED ARRIVAL, A YOUNG OFFICER WAS MET BY A GHASTLY TABLEAU.
ON THE FOURTH FLOOR LANDING LAY THE BODY OF NICHOLAS RYAN, HIS THROAT BRUTALLY SLASHED.
WHILE IN THEIR ROOM LAY HIS UNFORTUNATE SISTER, HER THROAT LIKEWISE CUT.
BOTH ROOM AND HALLWAY WERE BESOTTED WITH BLOOD!
BEFORE LONG, THE ENTIRE BUILDING WAS A HIVE OF CHAOTIC ACTIVITY.
THIS DID NOT SEEM TO BE A COMMON BURGLARY!

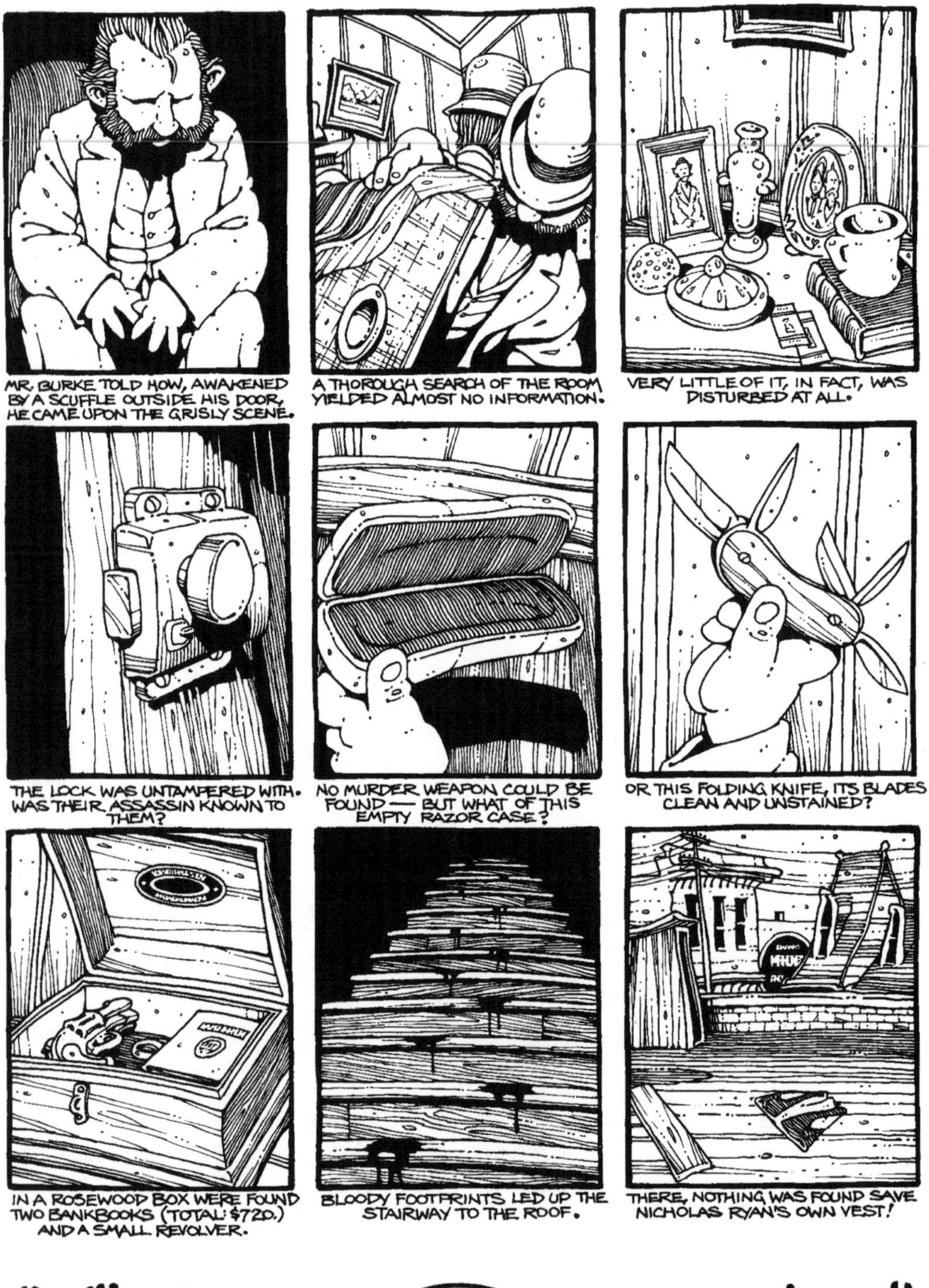
MR. BURKE TOLD HOW, AWAKENED BY A SCUFFLE OUTSIDE HIS DOOR, HE CAME UPON THE GRISLY SCENE.
A THOROUGH SEARCH OF THE ROOM YIELDED ALMOST NO INFORMATION.
VERY LITTLE OF IT, IN FACT, WAS DISTURBED AT ALL.
THE LOCK WAS UNTAMPERED WITH. WAS THEIR ASSASSIN KNOWN TO THEM?
NO MURDER WEAPON COULD BE FOUND — BUT WHAT OF THIS EMPTY RAZOR CASE?
OR THIS FOLDING KNIFE, ITS BLADES CLEAN AND UNSTAINED?
IN A ROSEWOOD BOX WERE FOUND TWO BANKBOOKS (TOTAL: $720.) AND A SMALL REVOLVER.
BLOODY FOOTPRINTS LED UP THE STAIRWAY TO THE ROOF.
THERE, NOTHING WAS FOUND SAVE NICHOLAS RYAN'S OWN VEST!

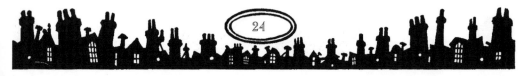

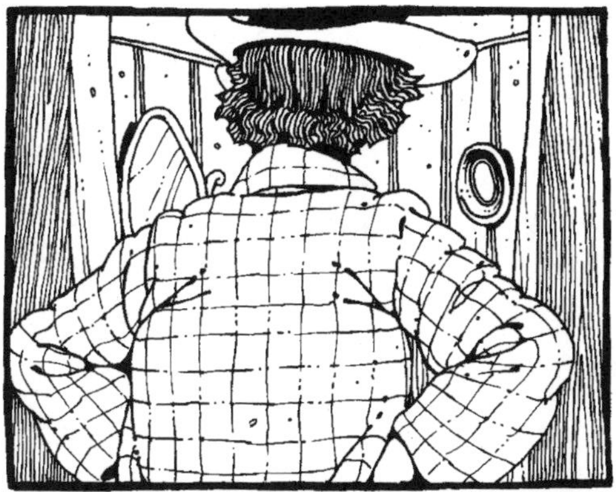

PATRICK RYAN, RESIDENT OF BROOKLYN AND BROTHER TO THE MURDERED PAIR, APPEARED AT THE SCENE.

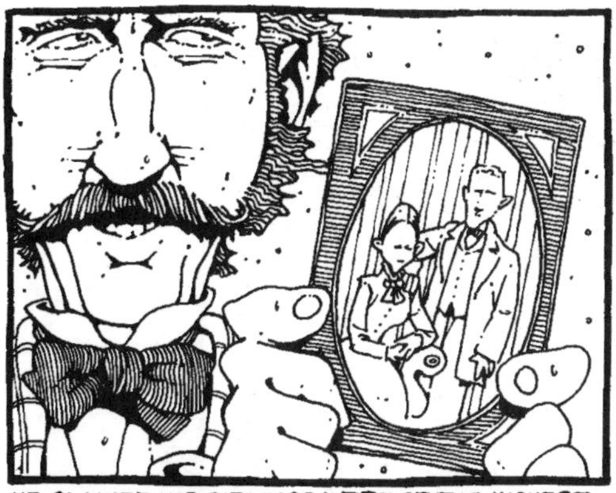

HE CLAIMED HIS SIBLINGS WERE OF THE HIGHEST CHRISTIAN CHARACTER AND COULD HAVE MADE ENEMIES OF NO ONE.

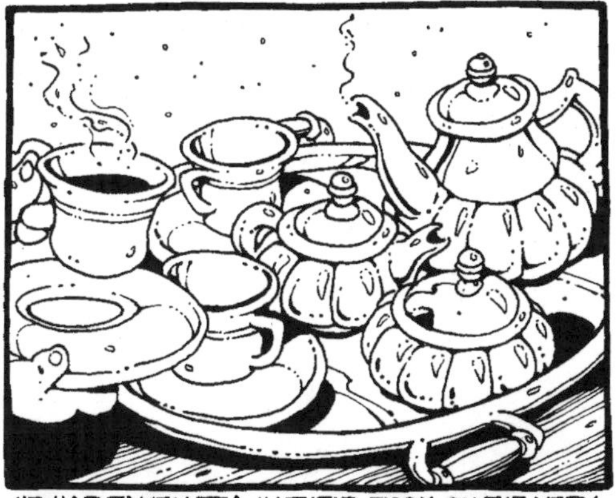

HE HAD TAKEN TEA IN THEIR ROOM ON THE VERY SUNDAY EVENING BEFORE THE TRAGEDY.

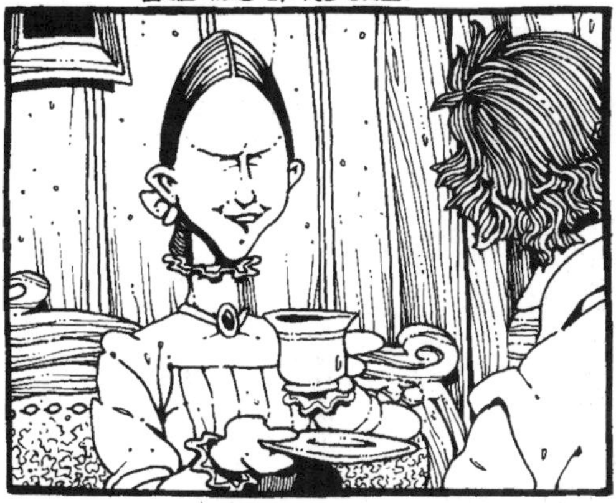

THEY HAD LAUGHED AND JOKED — ALL SEEMED WELL.

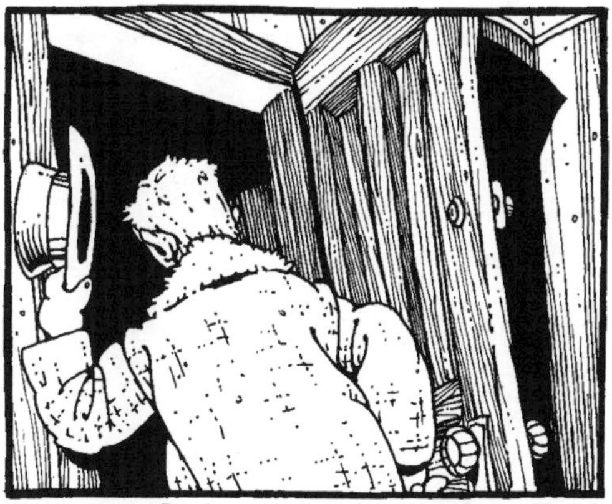

THEN NICHOLAS RYAN HAD SUDDENLY DEPARTED FOR AN UNEXPLAINED "APPOINTMENT."

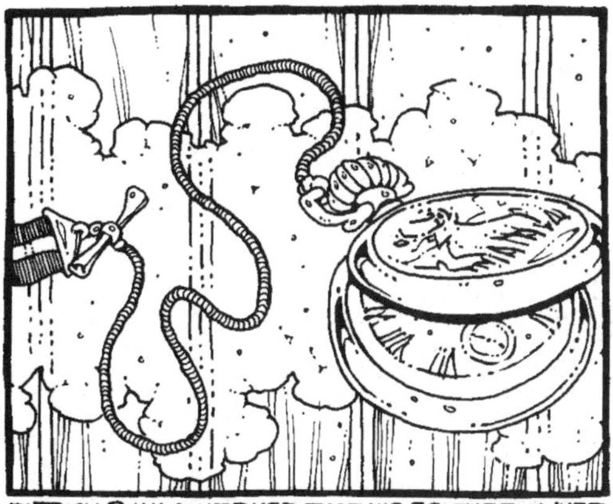

PATRICK RYAN CONFIRMED THAT HIS BROTHER OWNED A SILVER WATCH AND GOLD CHAIN — BUT NEITHER COULD BE FOUND AT THE MURDER SCENE.

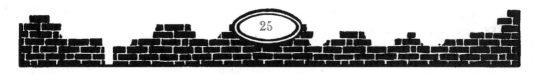

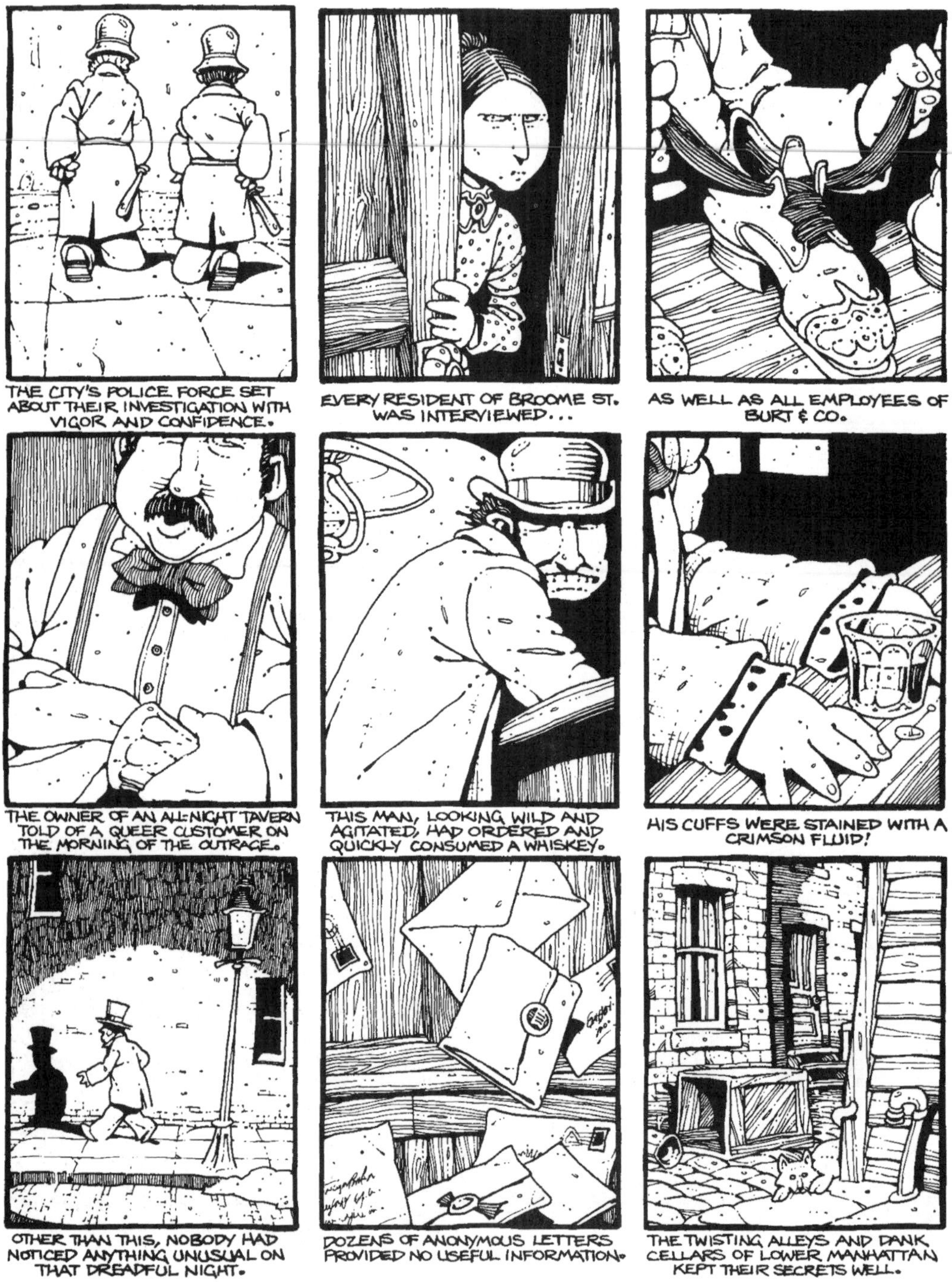
THE CITY'S POLICE FORCE SET ABOUT THEIR INVESTIGATION WITH VIGOR AND CONFIDENCE.
EVERY RESIDENT OF BROOME ST. WAS INTERVIEWED...
AS WELL AS ALL EMPLOYEES OF BURT & CO.
THE OWNER OF AN ALL-NIGHT TAVERN TOLD OF A QUEER CUSTOMER ON THE MORNING OF THE OUTRAGE.
THIS MAN, LOOKING WILD AND AGITATED, HAD ORDERED AND QUICKLY CONSUMED A WHISKEY.
HIS CUFFS WERE STAINED WITH A CRIMSON FLUID!
OTHER THAN THIS, NOBODY HAD NOTICED ANYTHING UNUSUAL ON THAT DREADFUL NIGHT.
DOZENS OF ANONYMOUS LETTERS PROVIDED NO USEFUL INFORMATION.
THE TWISTING ALLEYS AND DANK CELLARS OF LOWER MANHATTAN KEPT THEIR SECRETS WELL.

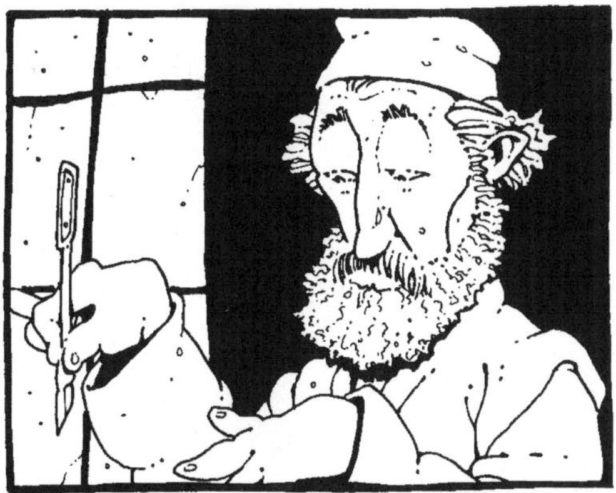

FURTHER COMPLICATING THE CASE: THE MEDICAL EXAMINER FOUND THAT MARY RYAN HAD BEEN WITH CHILD AT THE TIME OF HER DEATH.

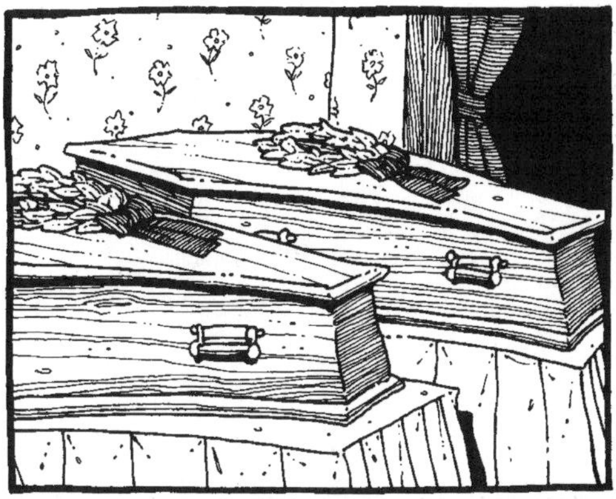

SO THREE PERSONS, NOT TWO, HAD MET THEIR FATES!

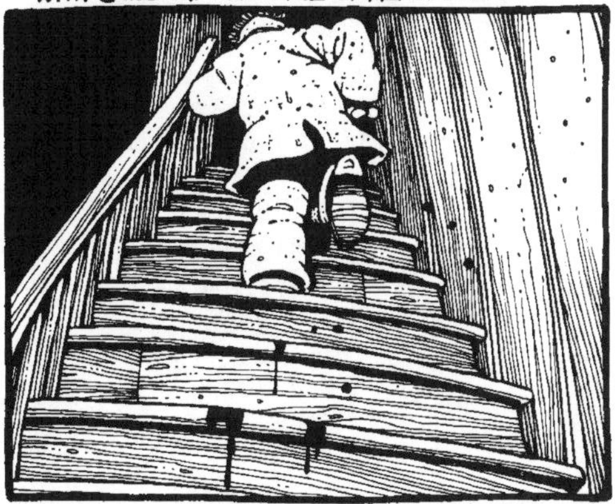

WHO WAS MARY RYAN'S LOVER, AND HAD THIS MAN, WISHING TO HIDE HIS TRANSGRESSION, COMMITTED THE DEED?

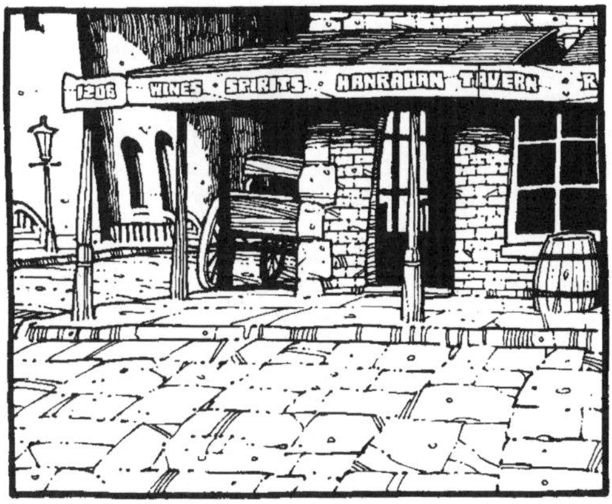
1206 WINES · SPIRITS · HANRAHAN TAVERN · R

(AND, AFTERWARD, STEADIED HIS NERVES AT THE CORNER TAVERN?)

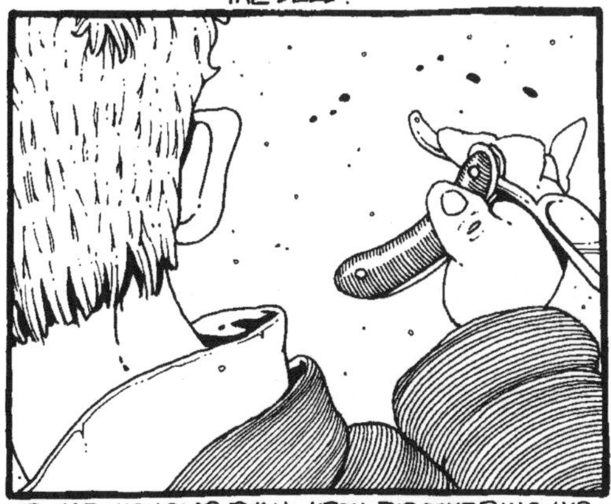

OR HAD NICHOLAS RYAN, UPON DISCOVERING HIS SISTER'S CONDITION, KILLED HER AND THEN HIMSELF OUT OF HIS RAGE AND SHAME?

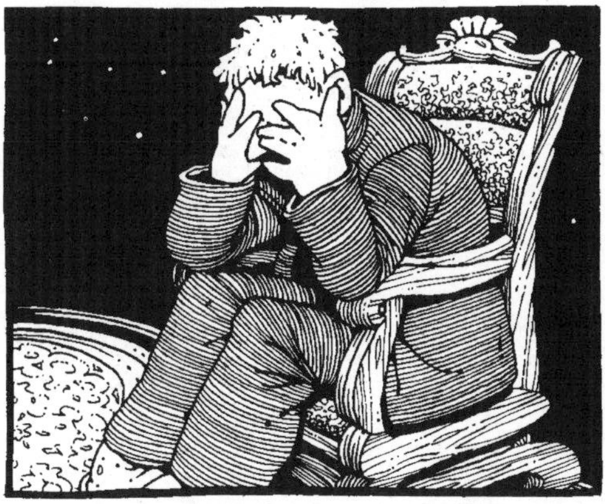

OR, EVEN MORE SHAMEFUL, WAS HE HIMSELF THE FATHER OF THE CHILD?

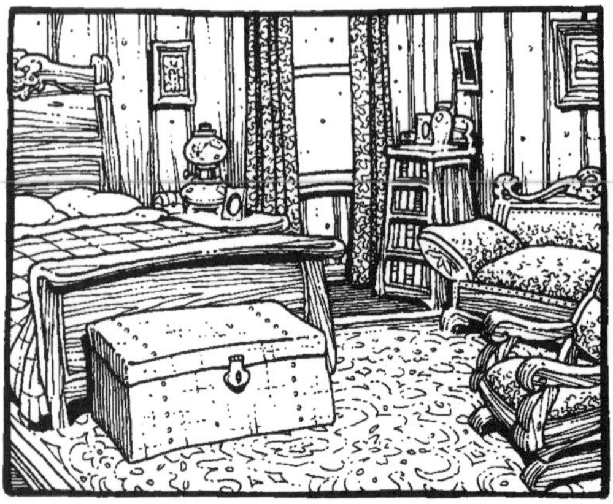

(YET, IF SO, WHY COULD NO WEAPON BE FOUND? AND WHERE WAS THE BROTHER'S SILVER WATCH?)

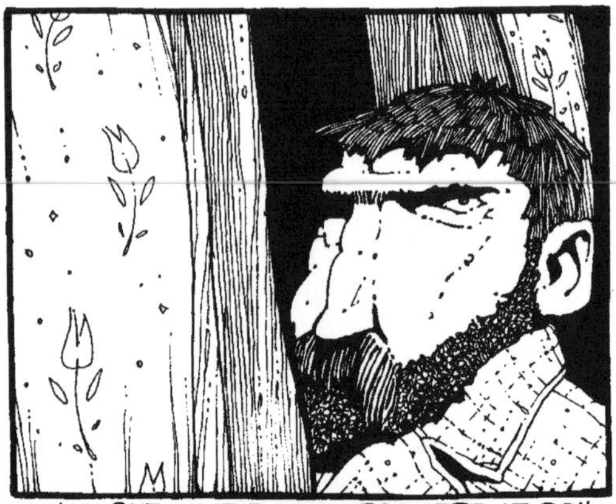

OR HAD ONE OF THE DARK ROOMERS AT 204 BROOME STREET SIMPLY GONE MAD AND SLASHED THE PAIR FOR SOME IMAGINED OFFENCE.

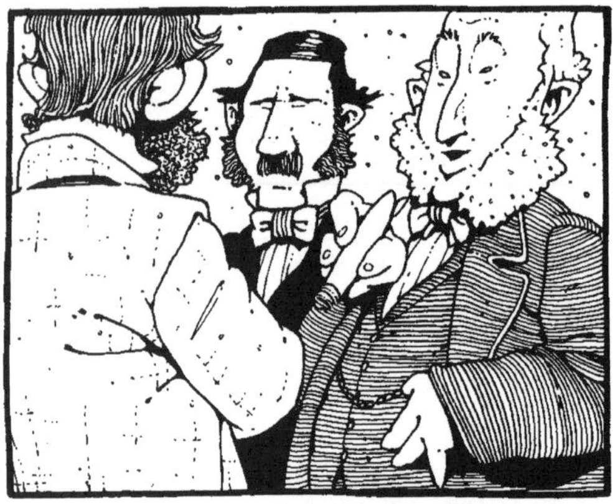

THE CASE EXCITED INTEREST AND SPECULATION IN THE CITY FOR SEVERAL DAYS.

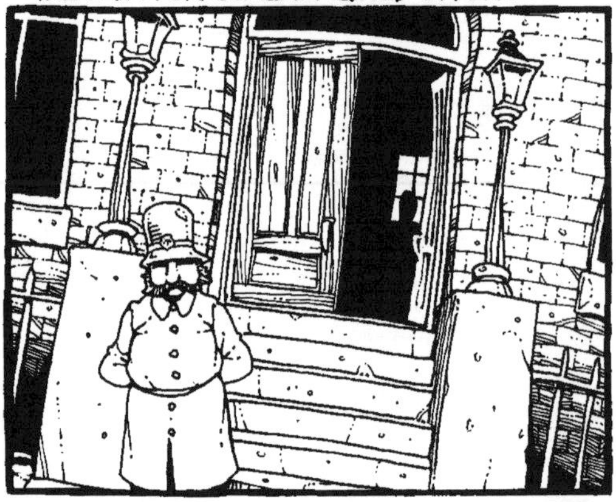

BUT, BEFORE LONG, A MANTLE OF HOPELESSNESS FELL OVER THE INVESTIGATION.

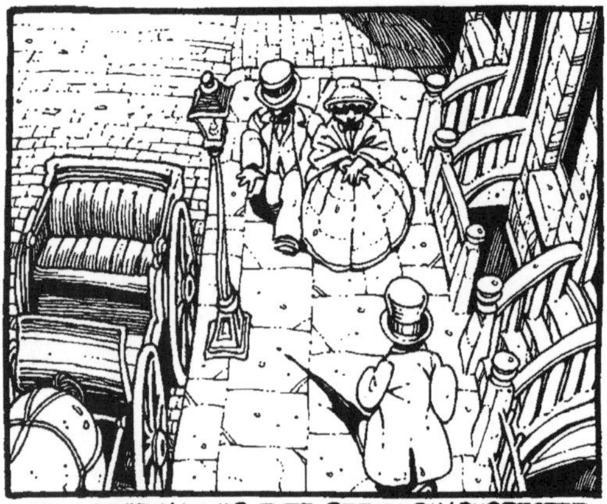

NO INDIVIDUAL WAS EVER SERIOUSLY SUSPECTED OF THE CRIME, LET ALONE ARRESTED.

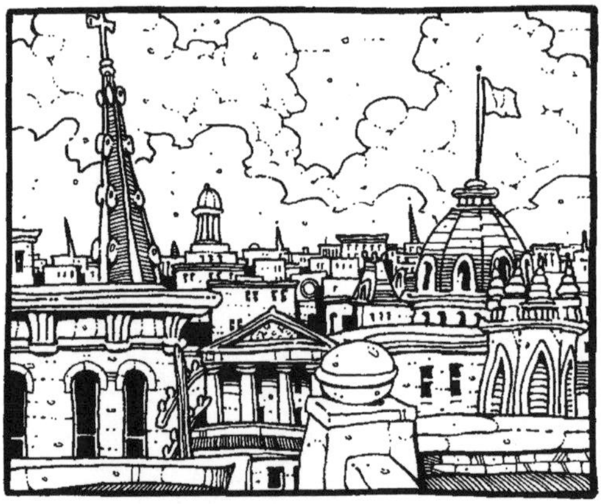

IT REMAINS A MYSTERY TO THIS DAY.

# THE CRIMES OF
# DR. E.W. PRITCHARD

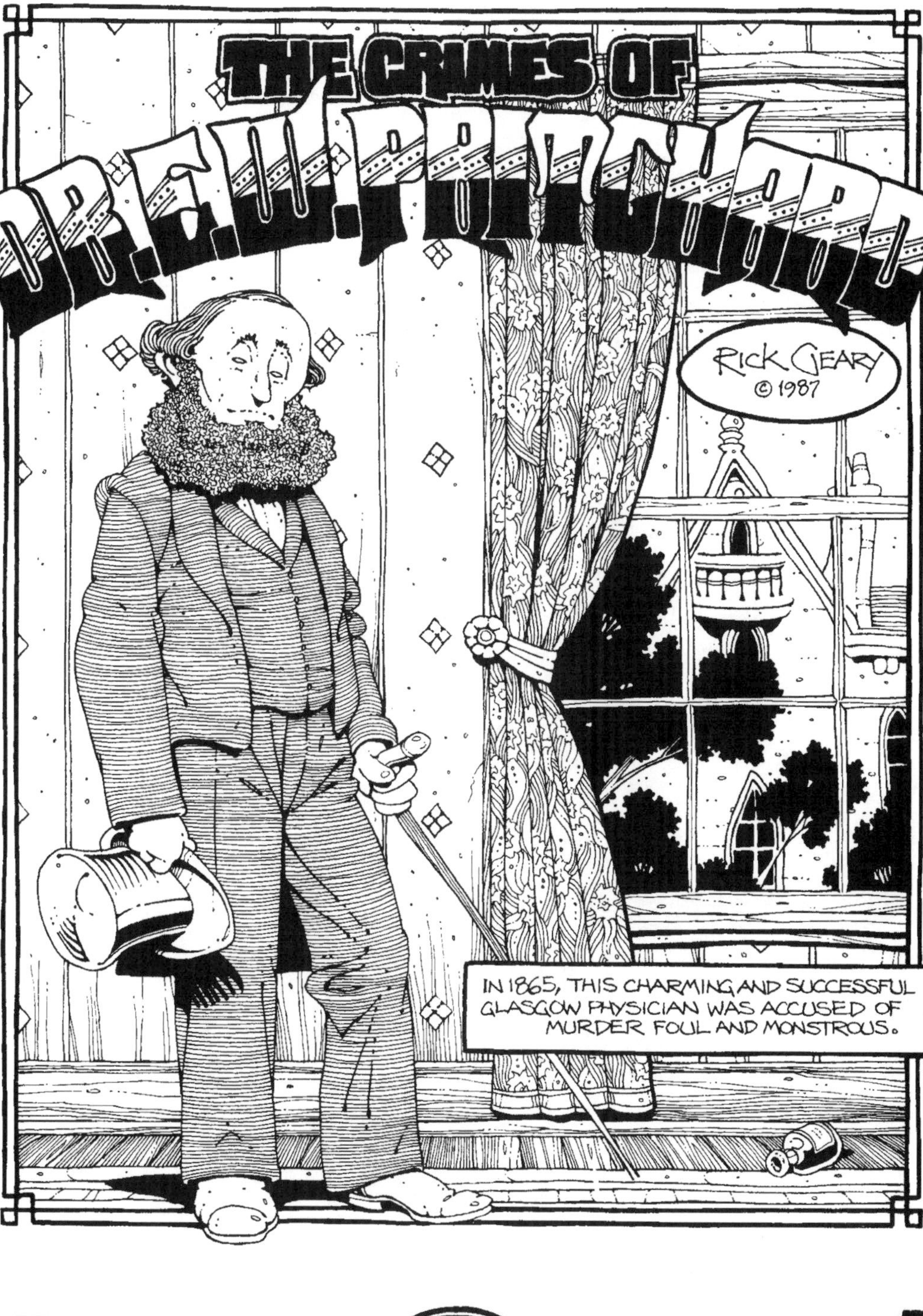
THE CRIMES OF
DR. E.W. PRITCHARD
RICK GEARY
© 1987
IN 1865, THIS CHARMING AND SUCCESSFUL GLASGOW PHYSICIAN WAS ACCUSED OF MURDER FOUL AND MONSTROUS.

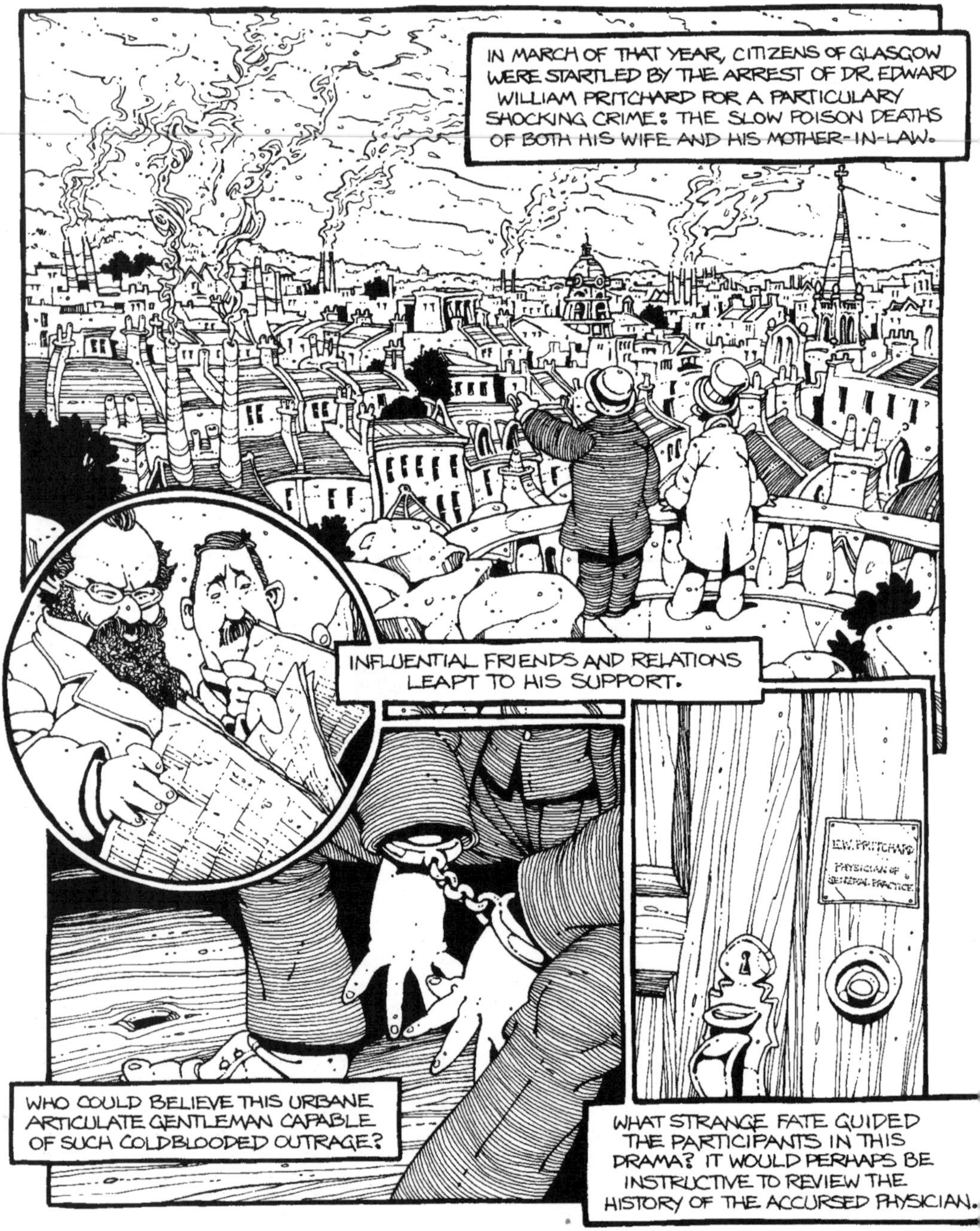
IN MARCH OF THAT YEAR, CITIZENS OF GLASGOW WERE STARTLED BY THE ARREST OF DR. EDWARD WILLIAM PRITCHARD FOR A PARTICULARY SHOCKING CRIME: THE SLOW POISON DEATHS OF BOTH HIS WIFE AND HIS MOTHER-IN-LAW.
INFLUENTIAL FRIENDS AND RELATIONS LEAPT TO HIS SUPPORT.
WHO COULD BELIEVE THIS URBANE ARTICULATE GENTLEMAN CAPABLE OF SUCH COLDBLOODED OUTRAGE?
E.W. PRITCHARD
PHYSICIAN OF GENERAL PRACTICE
WHAT STRANGE FATE GUIDED THE PARTICIPANTS IN THIS DRAMA? IT WOULD PERHAPS BE INSTRUCTIVE TO REVIEW THE HISTORY OF THE ACCURSED PHYSICIAN.

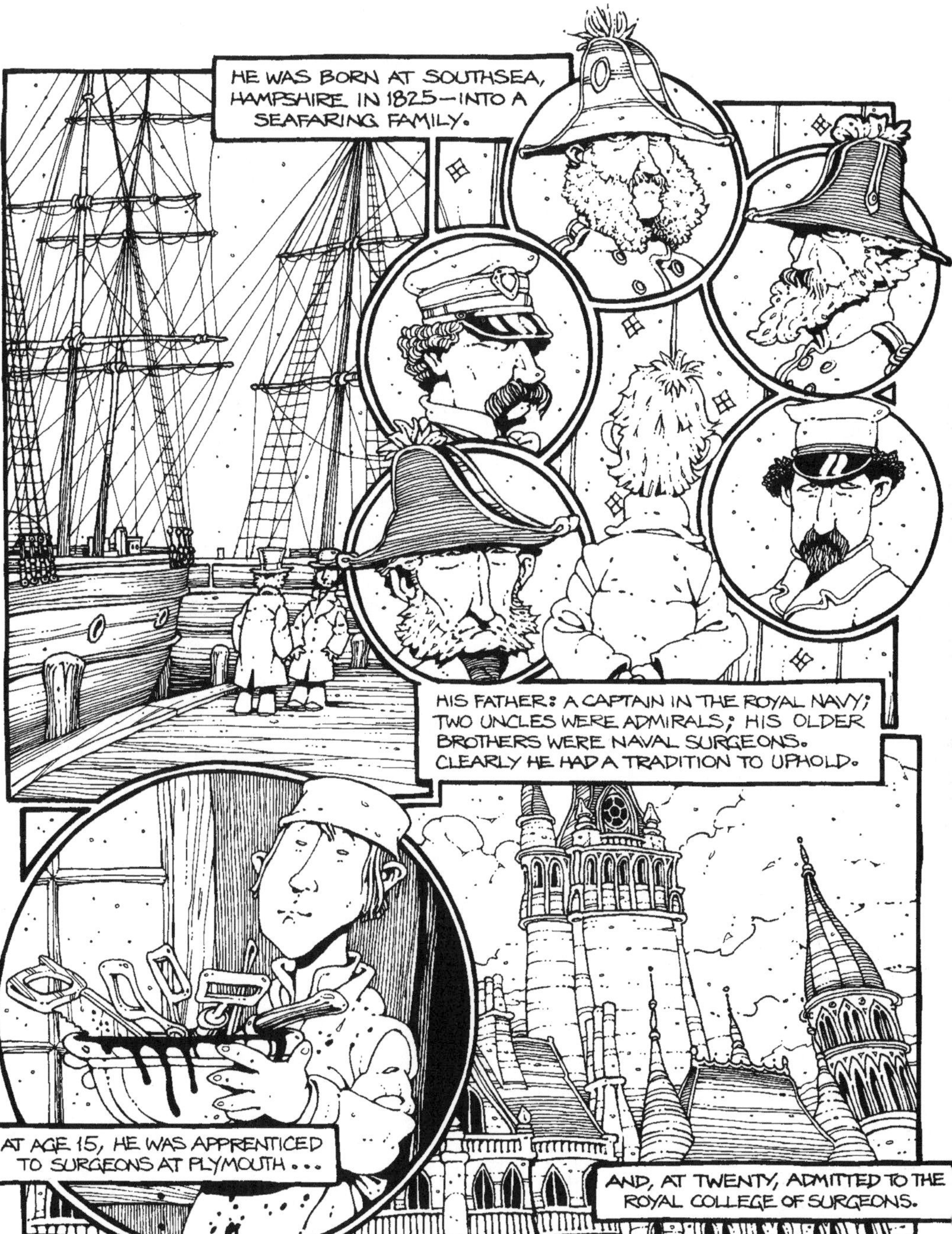
HE WAS BORN AT SOUTHSEA, HAMPSHIRE IN 1825—INTO A SEAFARING FAMILY.
HIS FATHER: A CAPTAIN IN THE ROYAL NAVY; TWO UNCLES WERE ADMIRALS; HIS OLDER BROTHERS WERE NAVAL SURGEONS. CLEARLY HE HAD A TRADITION TO UPHOLD.
AT AGE 15, HE WAS APPRENTICED TO SURGEONS AT PLYMOUTH...
AND, AT TWENTY, ADMITTED TO THE ROYAL COLLEGE OF SURGEONS.

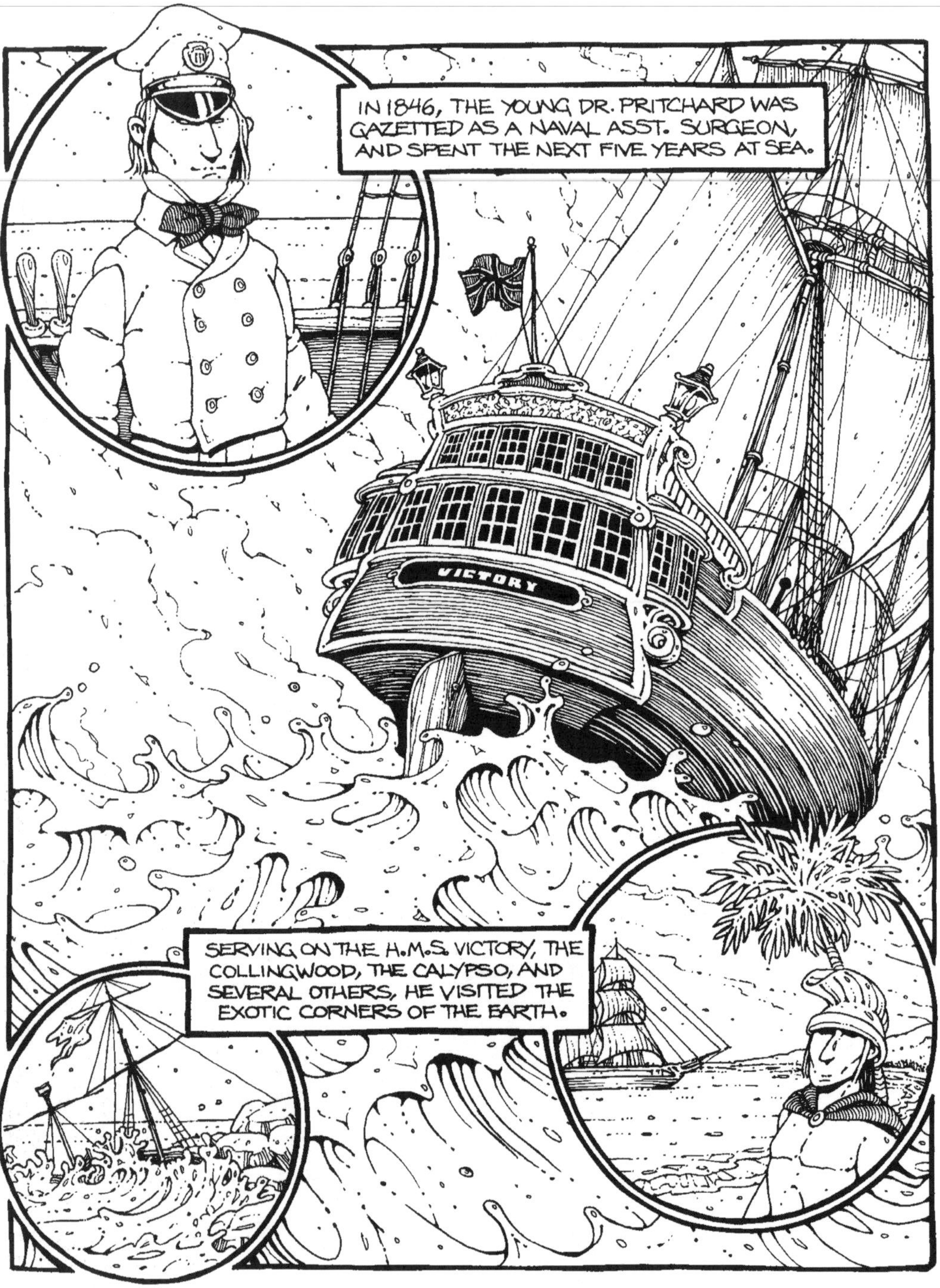
IN 1846, THE YOUNG DR. PRITCHARD WAS GAZETTED AS A NAVAL ASST. SURGEON, AND SPENT THE NEXT FIVE YEARS AT SEA.
VICTORY
SERVING ON THE H.M.S. VICTORY, THE COLLINGWOOD, THE CALYPSO, AND SEVERAL OTHERS, HE VISITED THE EXOTIC CORNERS OF THE EARTH.

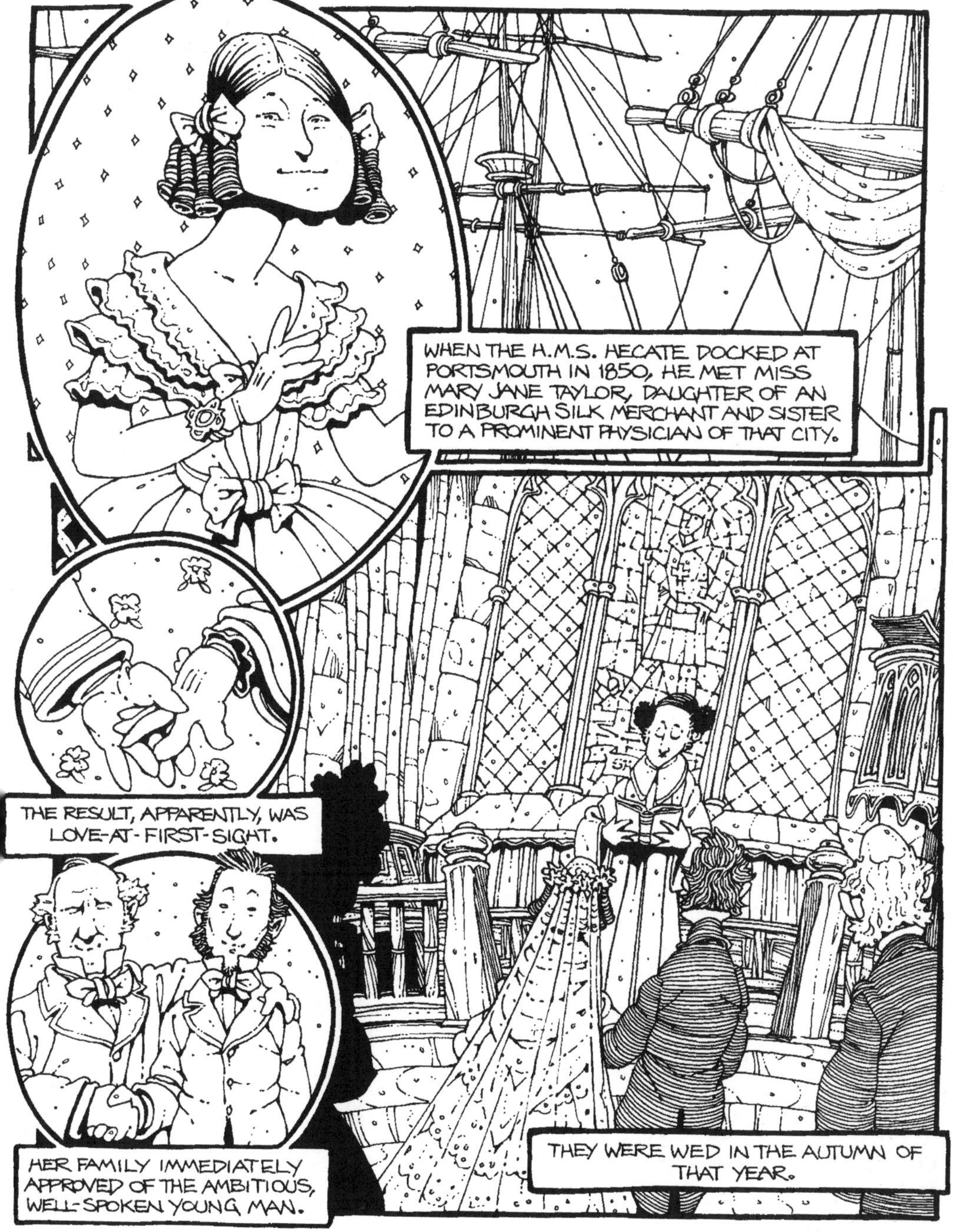
WHEN THE H.M.S. HECATE DOCKED AT PORTSMOUTH IN 1850, HE MET MISS MARY JANE TAYLOR, DAUGHTER OF AN EDINBURGH SILK MERCHANT AND SISTER TO A PROMINENT PHYSICIAN OF THAT CITY.
THE RESULT, APPARENTLY, WAS LOVE-AT-FIRST-SIGHT.
HER FAMILY IMMEDIATELY APPROVED OF THE AMBITIOUS, WELL-SPOKEN YOUNG MAN.
THEY WERE WED IN THE AUTUMN OF THAT YEAR.

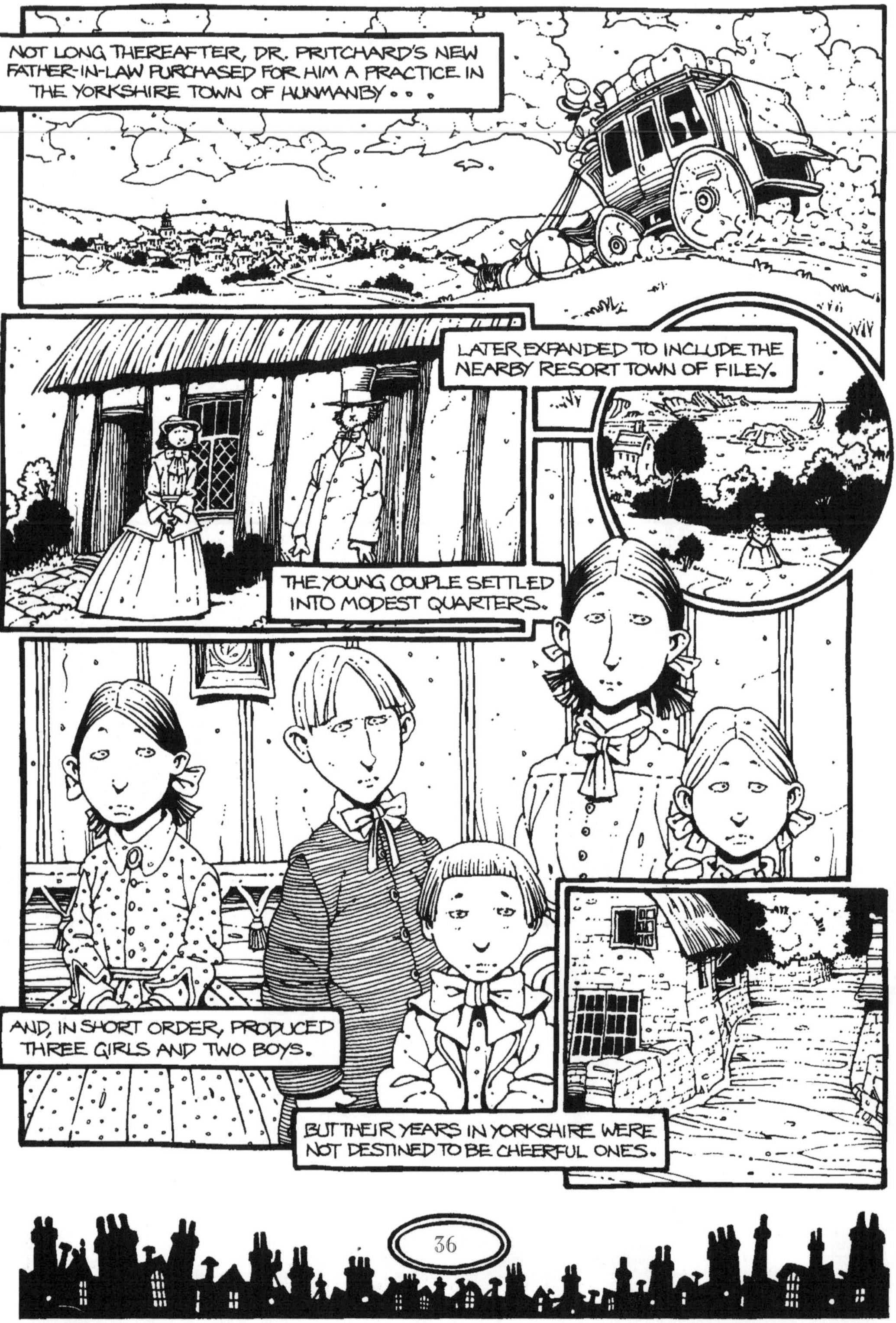
NOT LONG THEREAFTER, DR. PRITCHARD'S NEW FATHER-IN-LAW PURCHASED FOR HIM A PRACTICE IN THE YORKSHIRE TOWN OF HUNMANBY . . .
LATER EXPANDED TO INCLUDE THE NEARBY RESORT TOWN OF FILEY.
THE YOUNG COUPLE SETTLED INTO MODEST QUARTERS.
AND, IN SHORT ORDER, PRODUCED THREE GIRLS AND TWO BOYS.
BUT THEIR YEARS IN YORKSHIRE WERE NOT DESTINED TO BE CHEERFUL ONES.

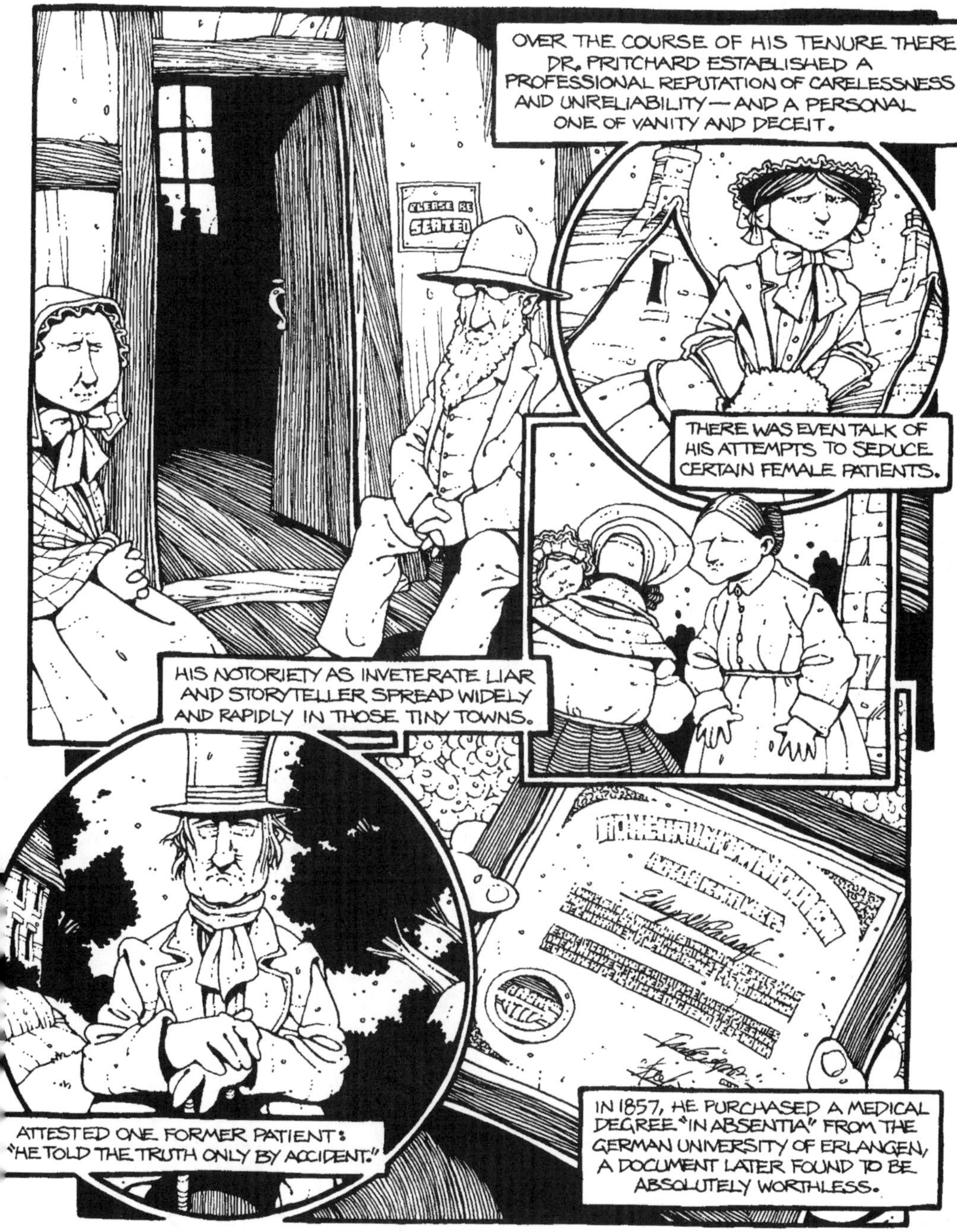
OVER THE COURSE OF HIS TENURE THERE DR. PRITCHARD ESTABLISHED A PROFESSIONAL REPUTATION OF CARELESSNESS AND UNRELIABILITY — AND A PERSONAL ONE OF VANITY AND DECEIT.
PLEASE BE SEATED
THERE WAS EVEN TALK OF HIS ATTEMPTS TO SEDUCE CERTAIN FEMALE PATIENTS.
HIS NOTORIETY AS INVETERATE LIAR AND STORYTELLER SPREAD WIDELY AND RAPIDLY IN THOSE TINY TOWNS.
ATTESTED ONE FORMER PATIENT: "HE TOLD THE TRUTH ONLY BY ACCIDENT."
IN 1857, HE PURCHASED A MEDICAL DEGREE "IN ABSENTIA" FROM THE GERMAN UNIVERSITY OF ERLANGEN, A DOCUMENT LATER FOUND TO BE ABSOLUTELY WORTHLESS.

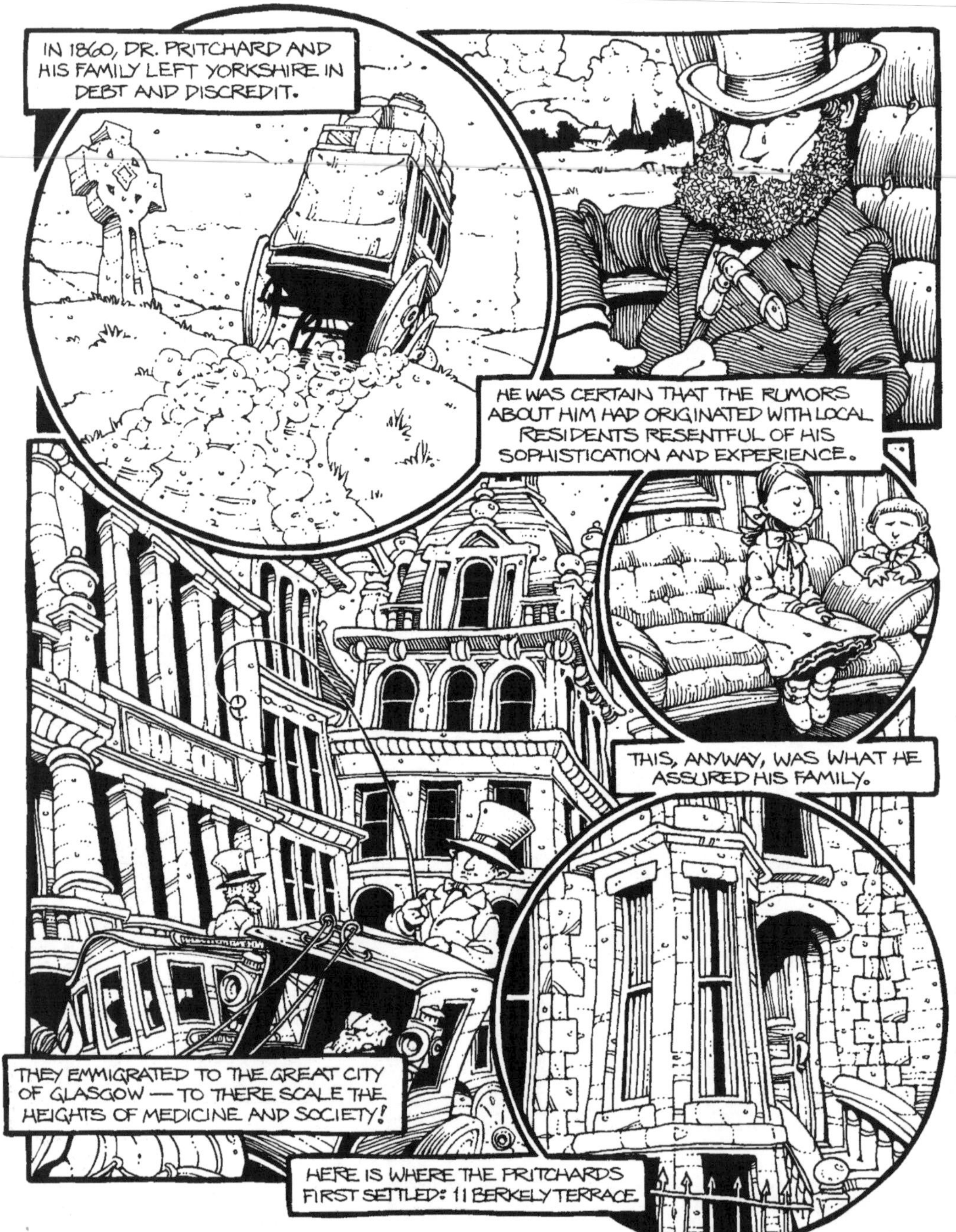
IN 1860, DR. PRITCHARD AND HIS FAMILY LEFT YORKSHIRE IN DEBT AND DISCREDIT.
HE WAS CERTAIN THAT THE RUMORS ABOUT HIM HAD ORIGINATED WITH LOCAL RESIDENTS RESENTFUL OF HIS SOPHISTICATION AND EXPERIENCE.
THIS, ANYWAY, WAS WHAT HE ASSURED HIS FAMILY.
ODEON
THEY EMMIGRATED TO THE GREAT CITY OF GLASGOW — TO THERE SCALE THE HEIGHTS OF MEDICINE AND SOCIETY!
HERE IS WHERE THE PRITCHARDS FIRST SETTLED: 11 BERKELY TERRACE.

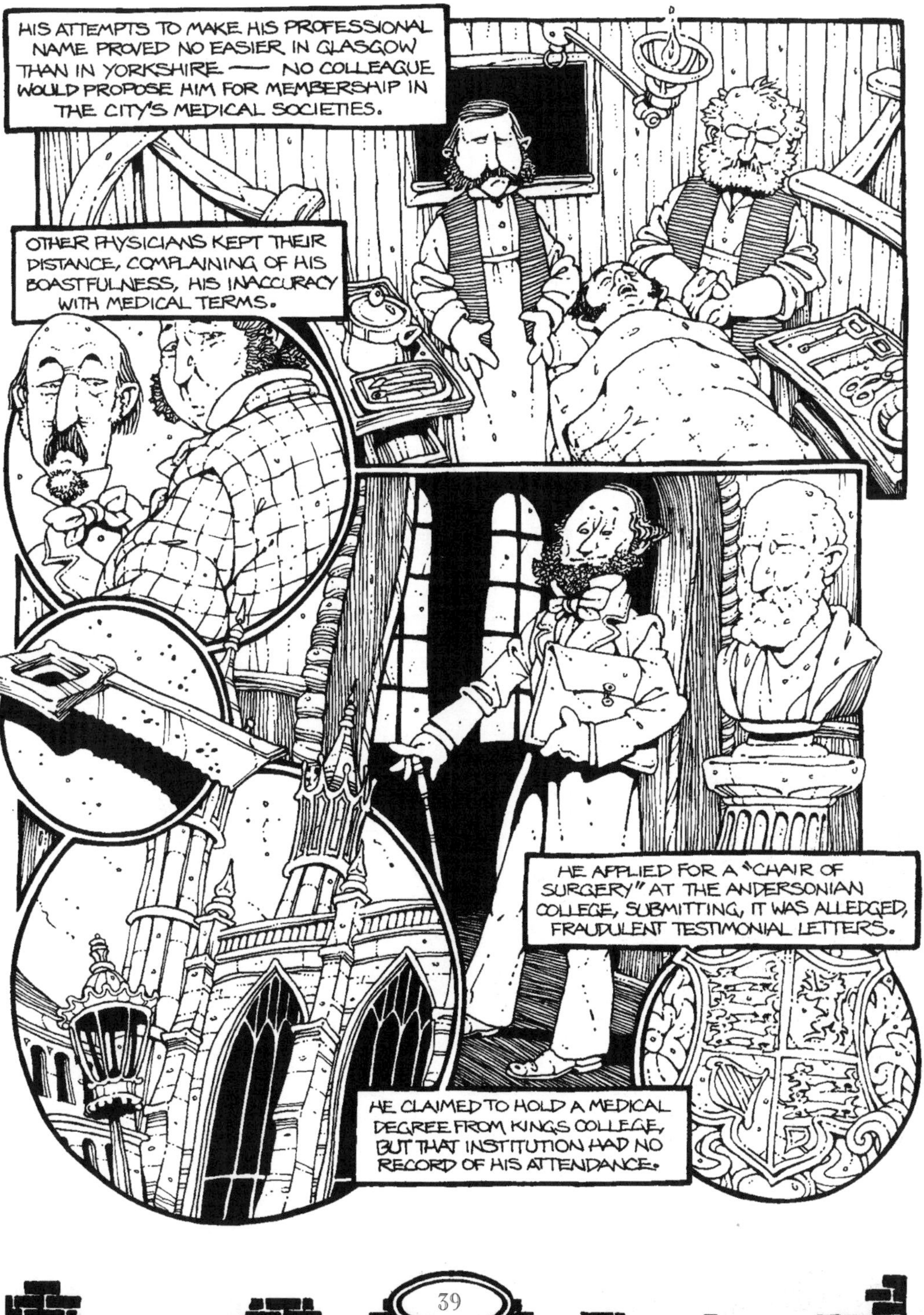
HIS ATTEMPTS TO MAKE HIS PROFESSIONAL NAME PROVED NO EASIER IN GLASGOW THAN IN YORKSHIRE — NO COLLEAGUE WOULD PROPOSE HIM FOR MEMBERSHIP IN THE CITY'S MEDICAL SOCIETIES.
OTHER PHYSICIANS KEPT THEIR DISTANCE, COMPLAINING OF HIS BOASTFULNESS, HIS INACCURACY WITH MEDICAL TERMS.
HE APPLIED FOR A "CHAIR OF SURGERY" AT THE ANDERSONIAN COLLEGE, SUBMITTING, IT WAS ALLEDGED, FRAUDULENT TESTIMONIAL LETTERS.
HE CLAIMED TO HOLD A MEDICAL DEGREE FROM KINGS COLLEGE, BUT THAT INSTITUTION HAD NO RECORD OF HIS ATTENDANCE.

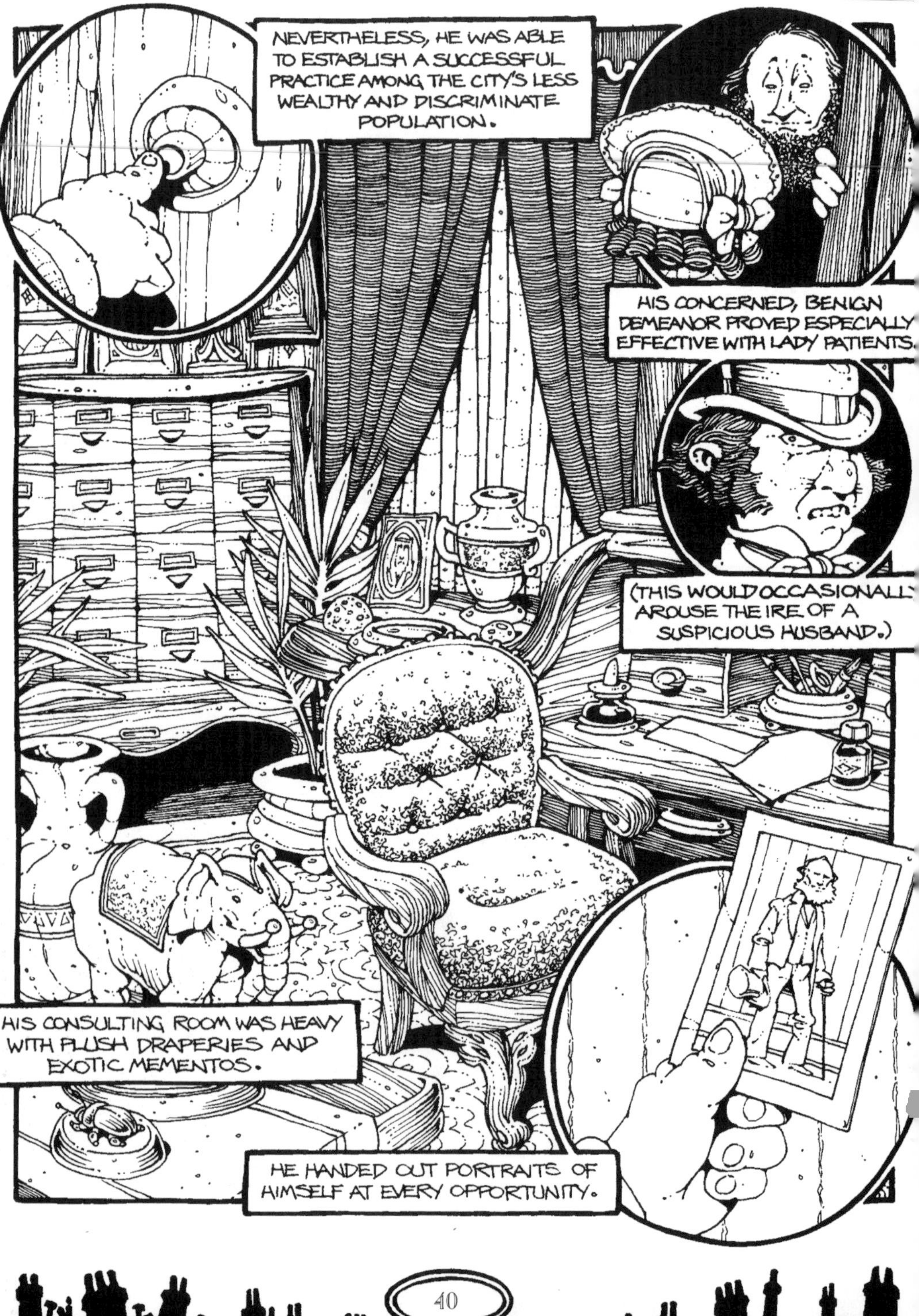
NEVERTHELESS, HE WAS ABLE TO ESTABLISH A SUCCESSFUL PRACTICE AMONG THE CITY'S LESS WEALTHY AND DISCRIMINATE POPULATION.
HIS CONCERNED, BENIGN DEMEANOR PROVED ESPECIALLY EFFECTIVE WITH LADY PATIENTS.
(THIS WOULD OCCASIONALLY AROUSE THE IRE OF A SUSPICIOUS HUSBAND.)
HIS CONSULTING ROOM WAS HEAVY WITH PLUSH DRAPERIES AND EXOTIC MEMENTOS.
HE HANDED OUT PORTRAITS OF HIMSELF AT EVERY OPPORTUNITY.

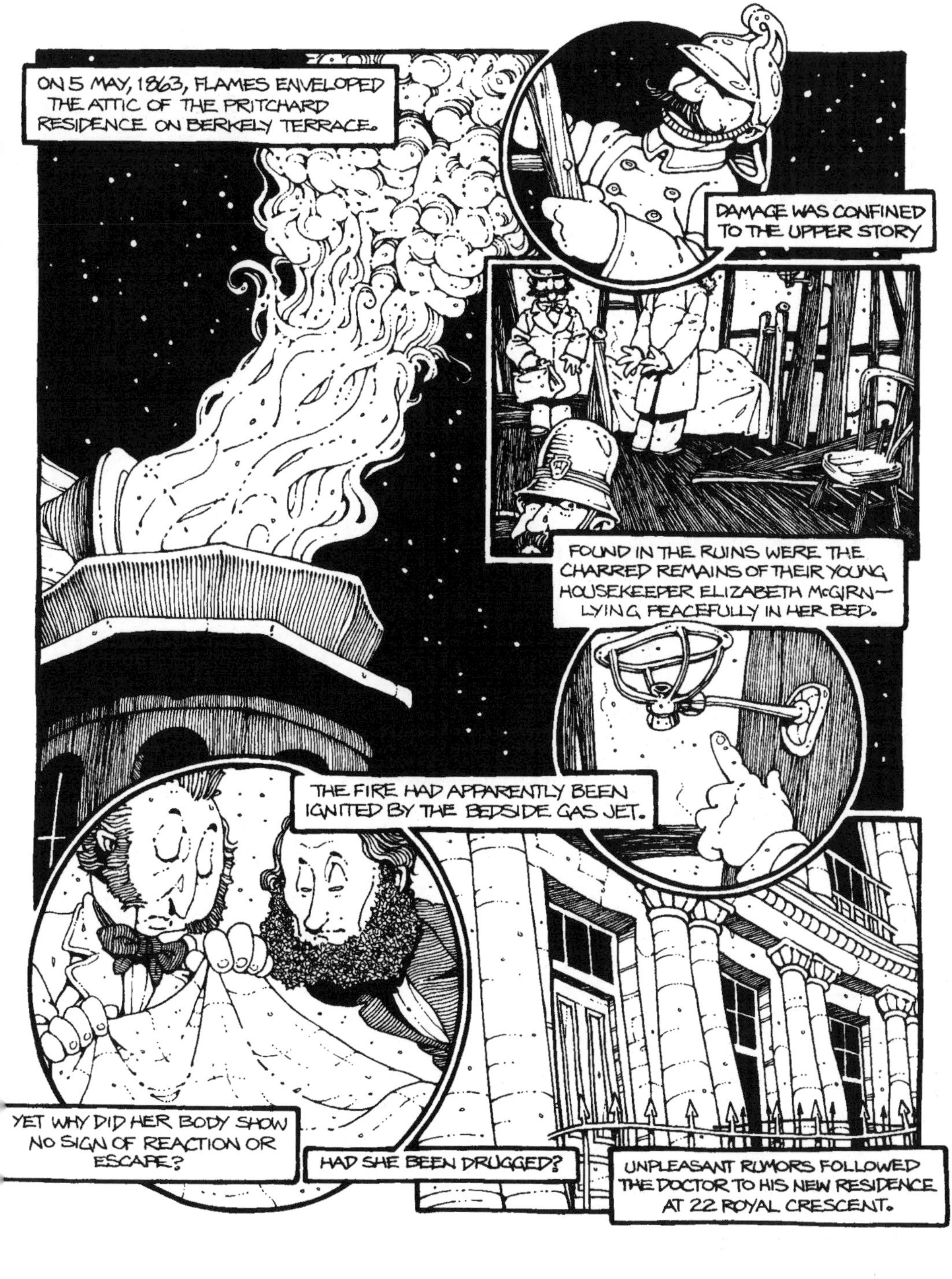
ON 5 MAY, 1863, FLAMES ENVELOPED THE ATTIC OF THE PRITCHARD RESIDENCE ON BERKELY TERRACE.
DAMAGE WAS CONFINED TO THE UPPER STORY
FOUND IN THE RUINS WERE THE CHARRED REMAINS OF THEIR YOUNG HOUSEKEEPER ELIZABETH McGIRN— LYING PEACEFULLY IN HER BED.
THE FIRE HAD APPARENTLY BEEN IGNITED BY THE BEDSIDE GAS JET.
YET WHY DID HER BODY SHOW NO SIGN OF REACTION OR ESCAPE?
HAD SHE BEEN DRUGGED?
UNPLEASANT RUMORS FOLLOWED THE DOCTOR TO HIS NEW RESIDENCE AT 22 ROYAL CRESCENT.

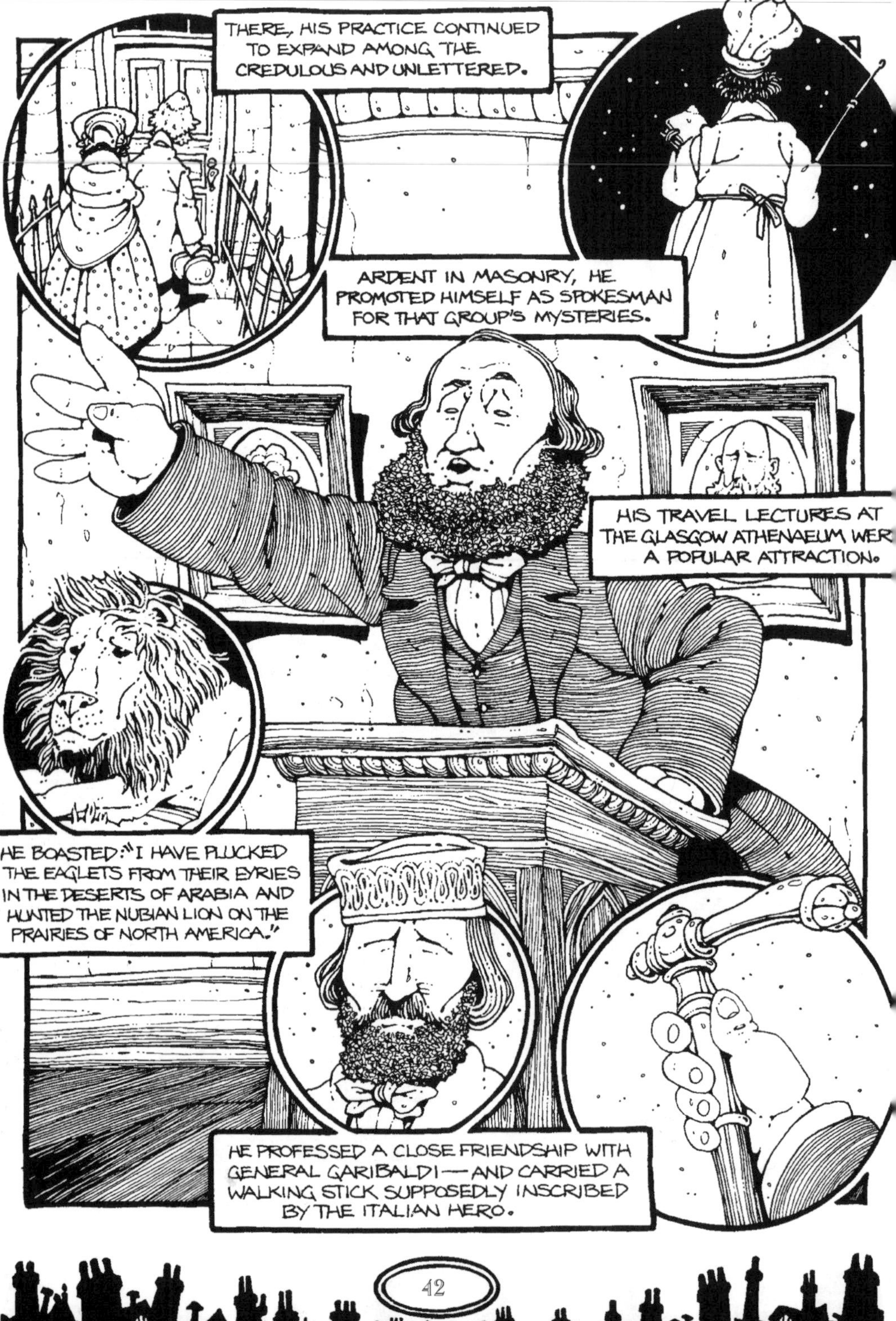
THERE, HIS PRACTICE CONTINUED TO EXPAND AMONG THE CREDULOUS AND UNLETTERED.
ARDENT IN MASONRY, HE PROMOTED HIMSELF AS SPOKESMAN FOR THAT GROUP'S MYSTERIES.
HIS TRAVEL LECTURES AT THE GLASGOW ATHENAEUM WER A POPULAR ATTRACTION.
HE BOASTED: "I HAVE PLUCKED THE EAGLETS FROM THEIR EYRIES IN THE DESERTS OF ARABIA AND HUNTED THE NUBIAN LION ON THE PRAIRIES OF NORTH AMERICA."
HE PROFESSED A CLOSE FRIENDSHIP WITH GENERAL GARIBALDI — AND CARRIED A WALKING STICK SUPPOSEDLY INSCRIBED BY THE ITALIAN HERO.

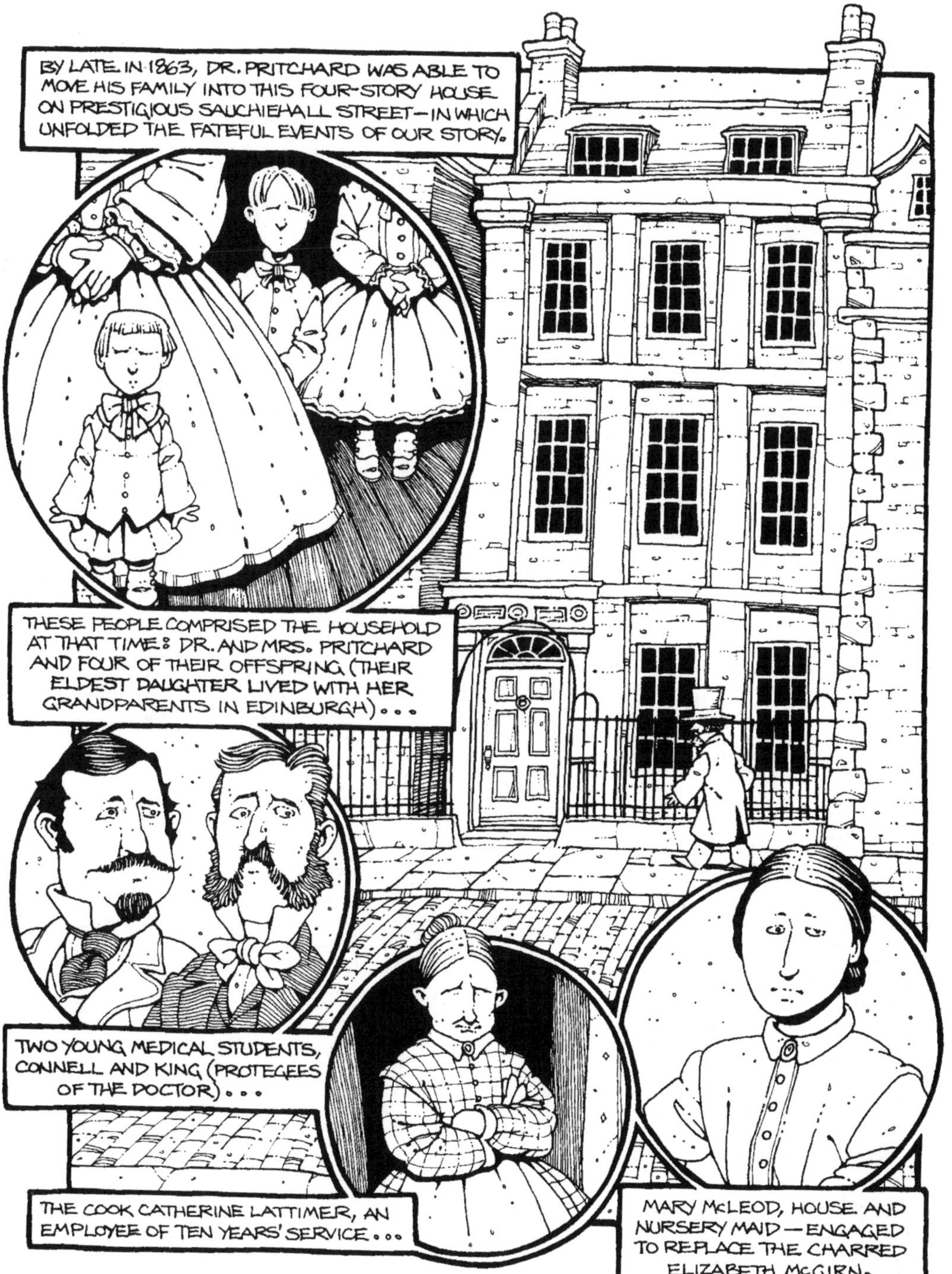
BY LATE IN 1863, DR. PRITCHARD WAS ABLE TO MOVE HIS FAMILY INTO THIS FOUR-STORY HOUSE ON PRESTIGIOUS SAUCHIEHALL STREET—IN WHICH UNFOLDED THE FATEFUL EVENTS OF OUR STORY.
THESE PEOPLE COMPRISED THE HOUSEHOLD AT THAT TIME: DR. AND MRS. PRITCHARD AND FOUR OF THEIR OFFSPRING (THEIR ELDEST DAUGHTER LIVED WITH HER GRANDPARENTS IN EDINBURGH)...
TWO YOUNG MEDICAL STUDENTS, CONNELL AND KING (PROTEGEES OF THE DOCTOR)...
THE COOK CATHERINE LATTIMER, AN EMPLOYEE OF TEN YEARS' SERVICE...
MARY McLEOD, HOUSE AND NURSERY MAID—ENGAGED TO REPLACE THE CHARRED ELIZABETH McGIRN.

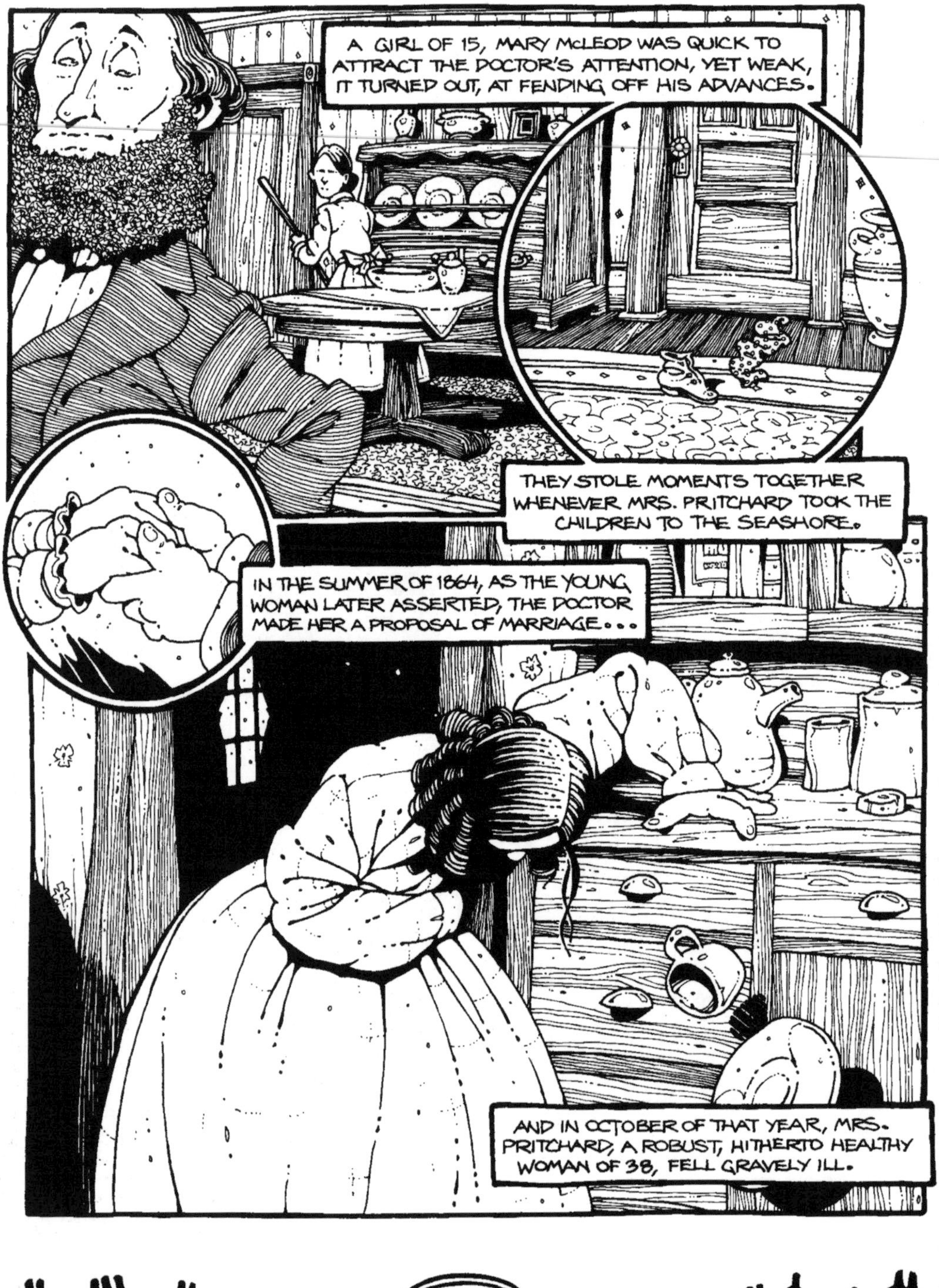
A GIRL OF 15, MARY McLEOD WAS QUICK TO ATTRACT THE DOCTOR'S ATTENTION, YET WEAK, IT TURNED OUT, AT FENDING OFF HIS ADVANCES.
THEY STOLE MOMENTS TOGETHER WHENEVER MRS. PRITCHARD TOOK THE CHILDREN TO THE SEASHORE.
IN THE SUMMER OF 1864, AS THE YOUNG WOMAN LATER ASSERTED, THE DOCTOR MADE HER A PROPOSAL OF MARRIAGE...
AND IN OCTOBER OF THAT YEAR, MRS. PRITCHARD, A ROBUST, HITHERTO HEALTHY WOMAN OF 38, FELL GRAVELY ILL.

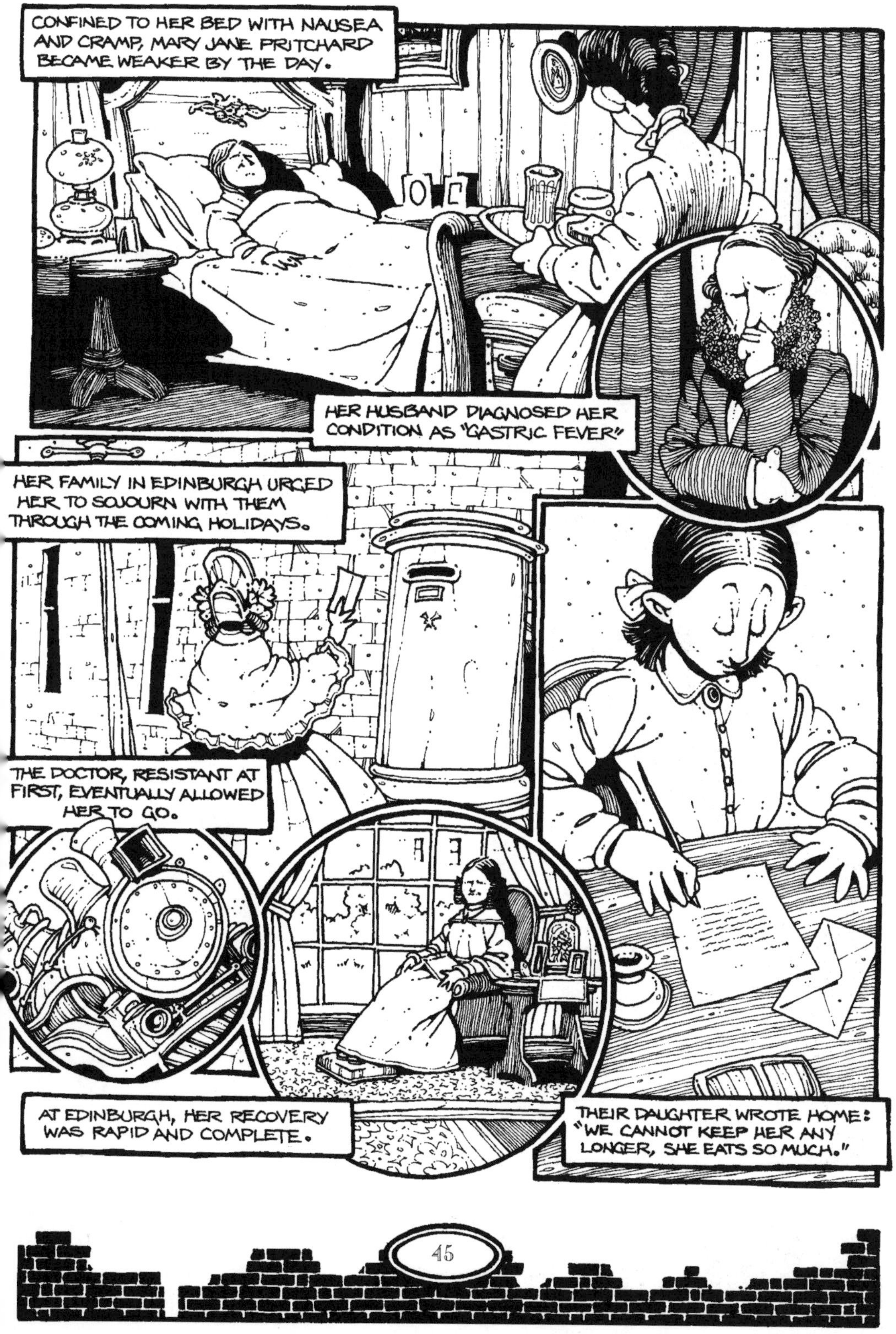
CONFINED TO HER BED WITH NAUSEA AND CRAMP, MARY JANE PRITCHARD BECAME WEAKER BY THE DAY.
HER HUSBAND DIAGNOSED HER CONDITION AS "GASTRIC FEVER"
HER FAMILY IN EDINBURGH URGED HER TO SOJOURN WITH THEM THROUGH THE COMING HOLIDAYS.
THE DOCTOR, RESISTANT AT FIRST, EVENTUALLY ALLOWED HER TO GO.
AT EDINBURGH, HER RECOVERY WAS RAPID AND COMPLETE.
THEIR DAUGHTER WROTE HOME: "WE CANNOT KEEP HER ANY LONGER, SHE EATS SO MUCH."

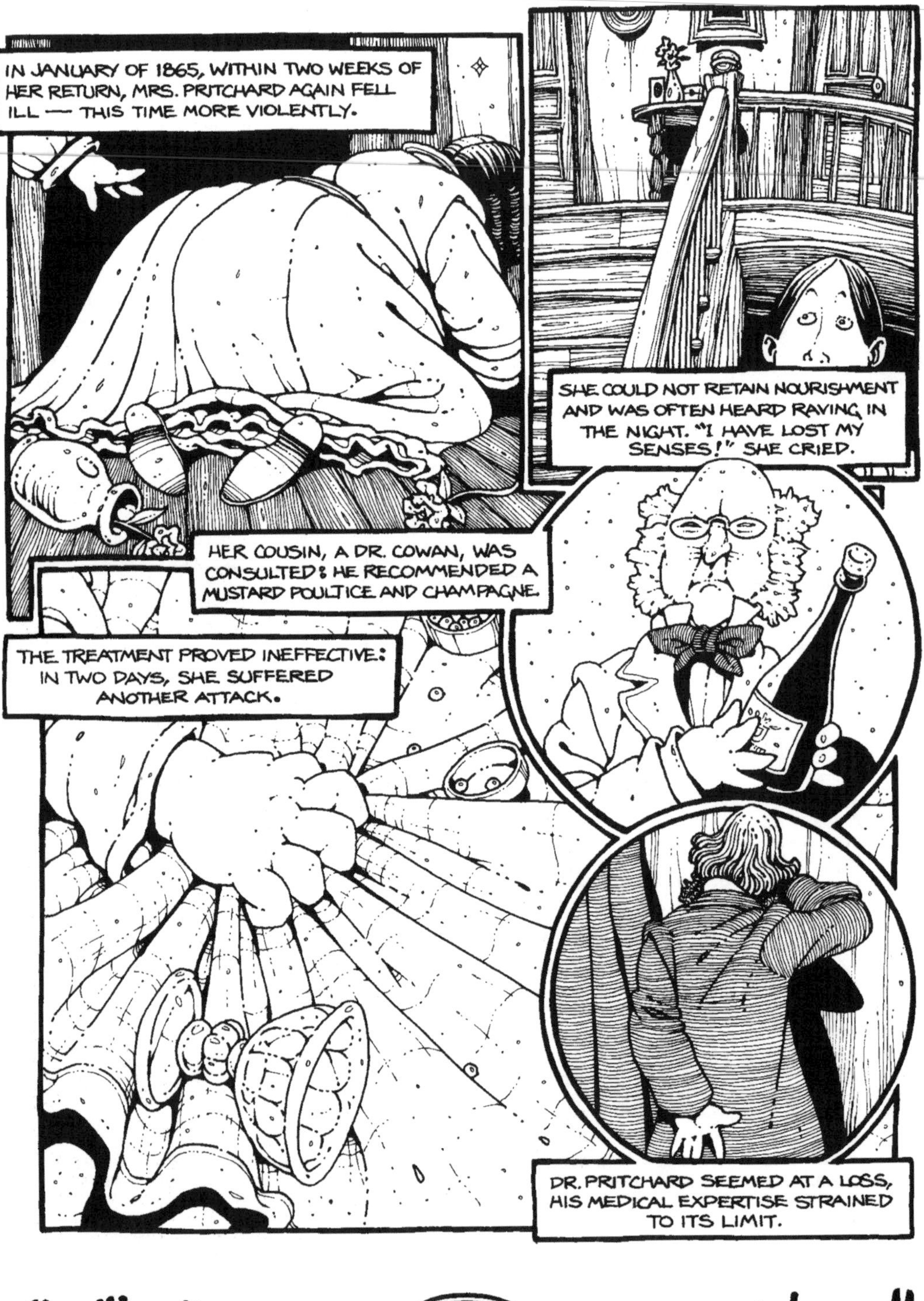
IN JANUARY OF 1865, WITHIN TWO WEEKS OF HER RETURN, MRS. PRITCHARD AGAIN FELL ILL — THIS TIME MORE VIOLENTLY.
SHE COULD NOT RETAIN NOURISHMENT AND WAS OFTEN HEARD RAVING IN THE NIGHT. "I HAVE LOST MY SENSES!" SHE CRIED.
HER COUSIN, A DR. COWAN, WAS CONSULTED: HE RECOMMENDED A MUSTARD POULTICE AND CHAMPAGNE.
THE TREATMENT PROVED INEFFECTIVE: IN TWO DAYS, SHE SUFFERED ANOTHER ATTACK.
DR. PRITCHARD SEEMED AT A LOSS, HIS MEDICAL EXPERTISE STRAINED TO ITS LIMIT.

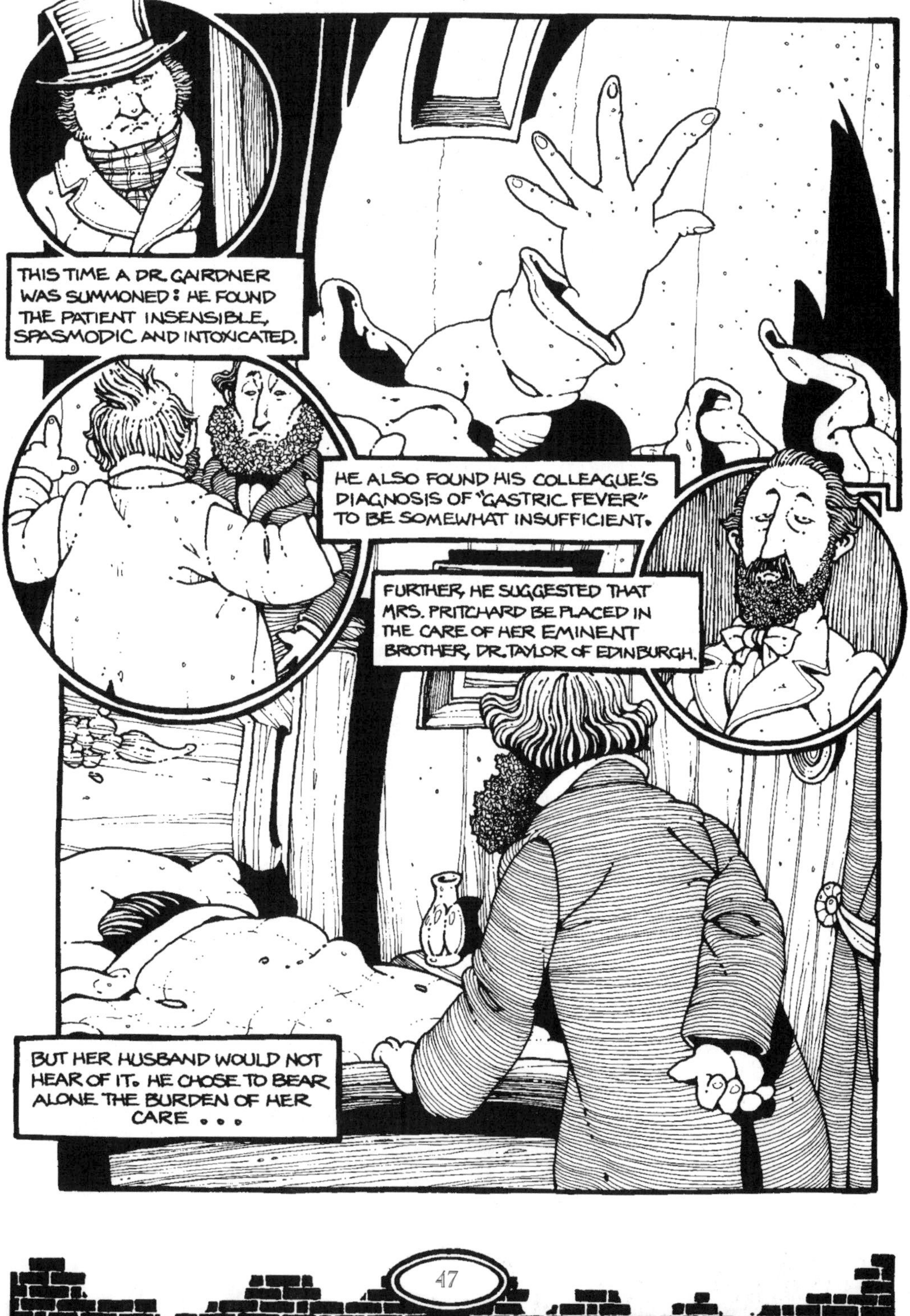
THIS TIME A DR. GAIRDNER WAS SUMMONED: HE FOUND THE PATIENT INSENSIBLE, SPASMODIC AND INTOXICATED.
HE ALSO FOUND HIS COLLEAGUE'S DIAGNOSIS OF "GASTRIC FEVER" TO BE SOMEWHAT INSUFFICIENT.
FURTHER, HE SUGGESTED THAT MRS. PRITCHARD BE PLACED IN THE CARE OF HER EMINENT BROTHER, DR. TAYLOR OF EDINBURGH.
BUT HER HUSBAND WOULD NOT HEAR OF IT. HE CHOSE TO BEAR ALONE THE BURDEN OF HER CARE . . .

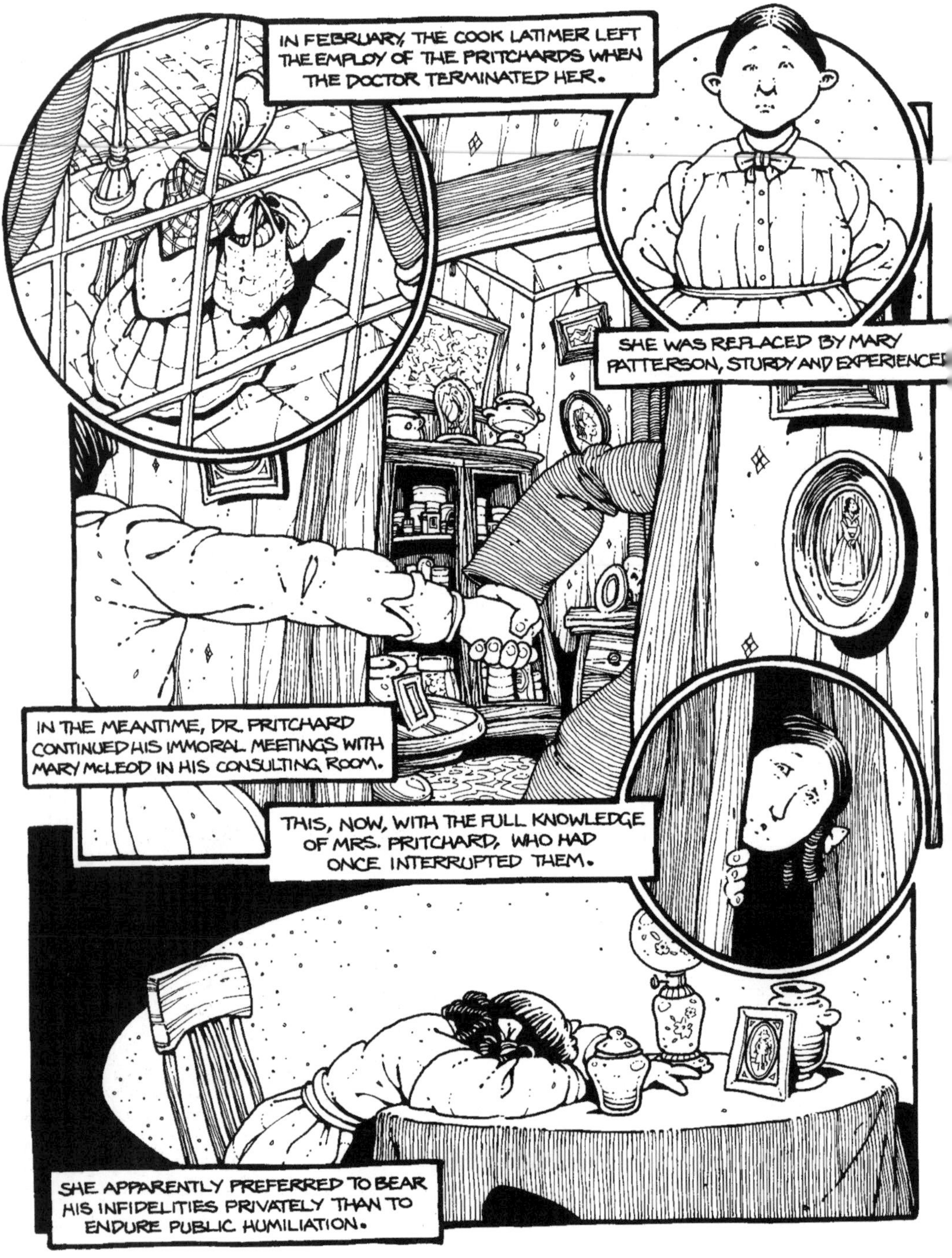
IN FEBRUARY, THE COOK LATIMER LEFT THE EMPLOY OF THE PRITCHARDS WHEN THE DOCTOR TERMINATED HER.
SHE WAS REPLACED BY MARY PATTERSON, STURDY AND EXPERIENCED.
IN THE MEANTIME, DR. PRITCHARD CONTINUED HIS IMMORAL MEETINGS WITH MARY McLEOD IN HIS CONSULTING ROOM.
THIS, NOW, WITH THE FULL KNOWLEDGE OF MRS. PRITCHARD, WHO HAD ONCE INTERRUPTED THEM.
SHE APPARENTLY PREFERRED TO BEAR HIS INFIDELITIES PRIVATELY THAN TO ENDURE PUBLIC HUMILIATION.

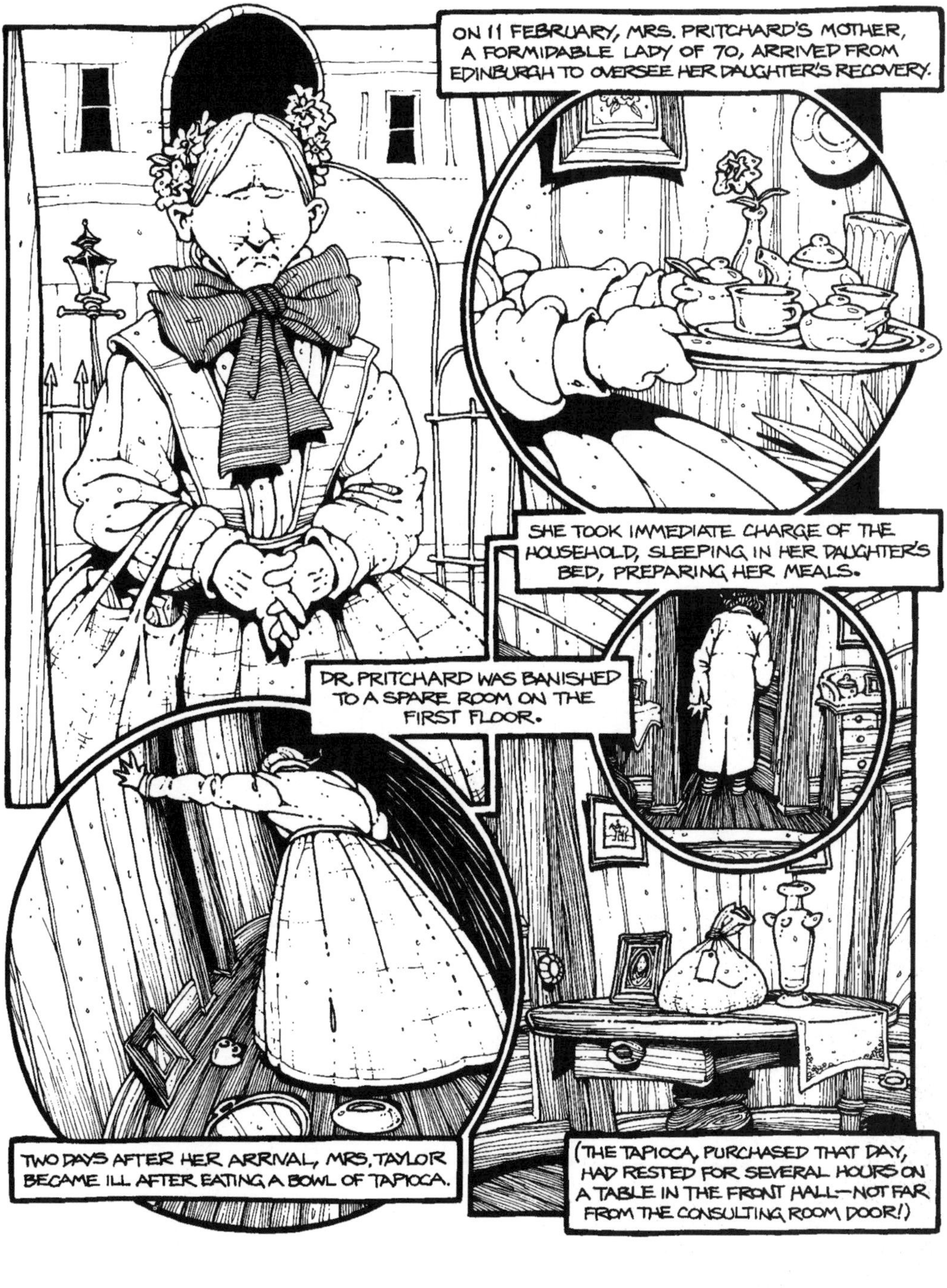
ON 11 FEBRUARY, MRS. PRITCHARD'S MOTHER, A FORMIDABLE LADY OF 70, ARRIVED FROM EDINBURGH TO OVERSEE HER DAUGHTER'S RECOVERY.
SHE TOOK IMMEDIATE CHARGE OF THE HOUSEHOLD, SLEEPING IN HER DAUGHTER'S BED, PREPARING HER MEALS.
DR. PRITCHARD WAS BANISHED TO A SPARE ROOM ON THE FIRST FLOOR.
TWO DAYS AFTER HER ARRIVAL, MRS. TAYLOR BECAME ILL AFTER EATING A BOWL OF TAPIOCA.
(THE TAPIOCA, PURCHASED THAT DAY, HAD RESTED FOR SEVERAL HOURS ON A TABLE IN THE FRONT HALL—NOT FAR FROM THE CONSULTING ROOM DOOR!)

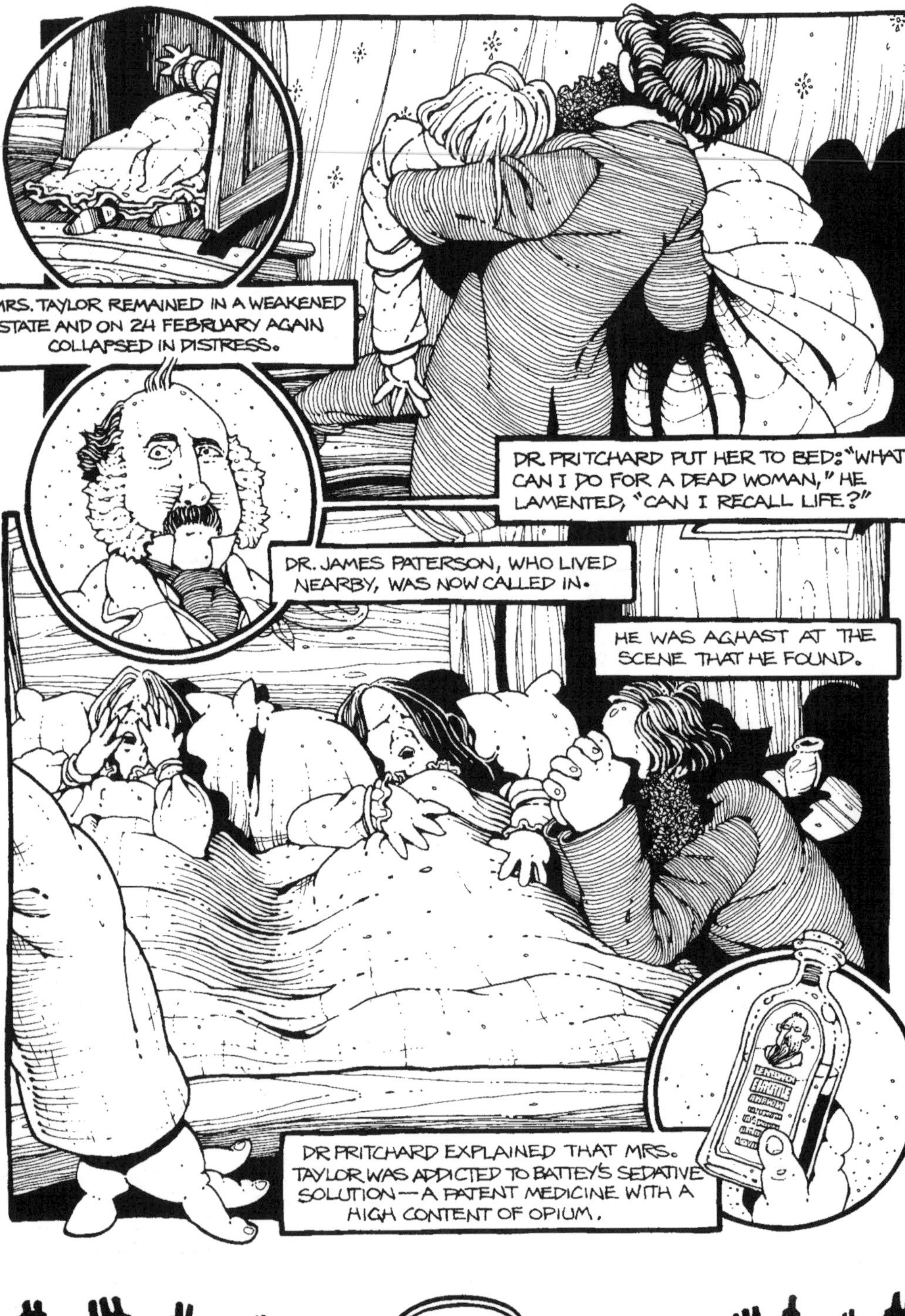
MRS. TAYLOR REMAINED IN A WEAKENED STATE AND ON 24 FEBRUARY AGAIN COLLAPSED IN DISTRESS.
DR. PRITCHARD PUT HER TO BED: "WHAT CAN I DO FOR A DEAD WOMAN," HE LAMENTED, "CAN I RECALL LIFE?"
DR. JAMES PATERSON, WHO LIVED NEARBY, WAS NOW CALLED IN.
HE WAS AGHAST AT THE SCENE THAT HE FOUND.
DR PRITCHARD EXPLAINED THAT MRS. TAYLOR WAS ADDICTED TO BATTEY'S SEDATIVE SOLUTION—A PATENT MEDICINE WITH A HIGH CONTENT OF OPIUM.

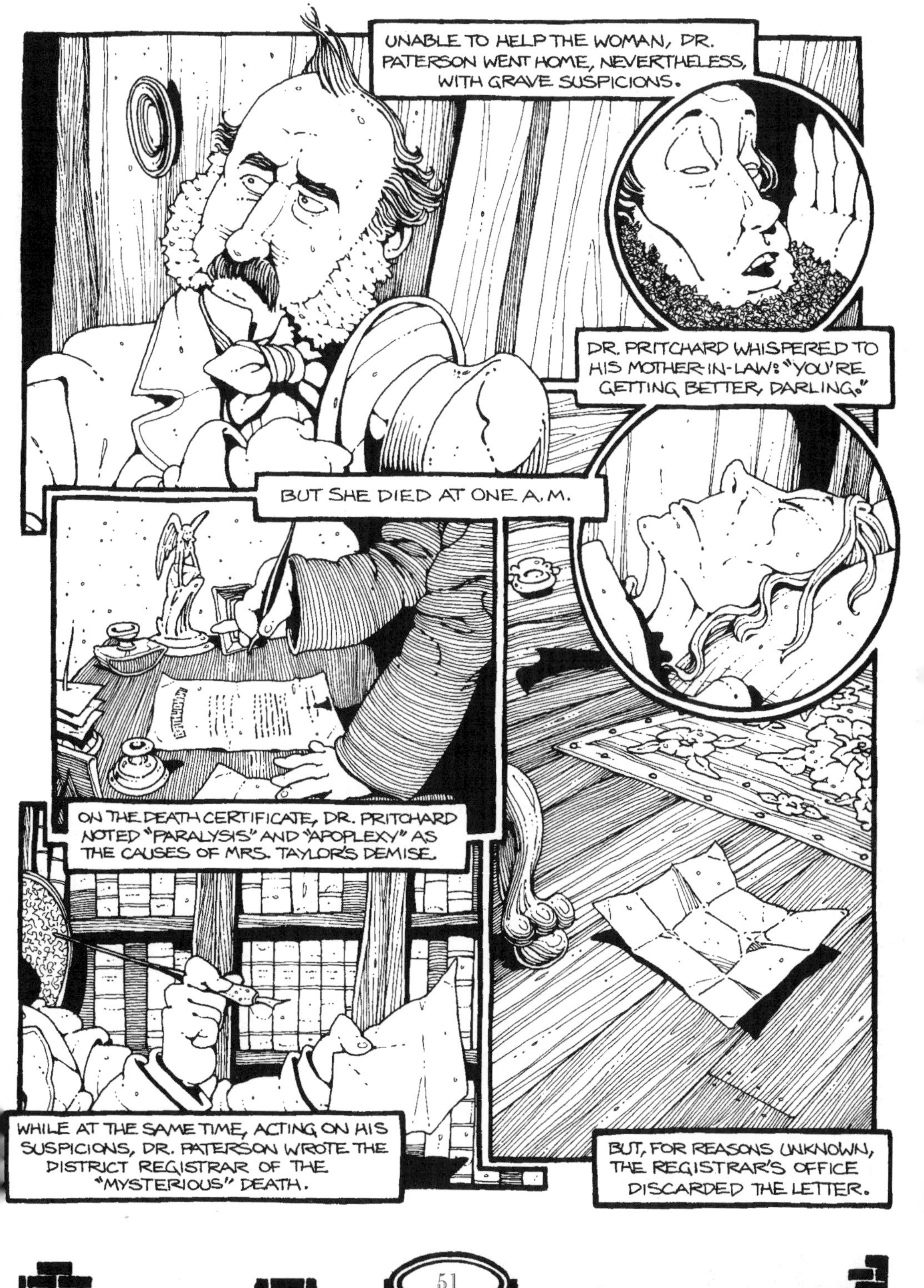
UNABLE TO HELP THE WOMAN, DR. PATERSON WENT HOME, NEVERTHELESS, WITH GRAVE SUSPICIONS.
DR. PRITCHARD WHISPERED TO HIS MOTHER-IN-LAW: "YOU'RE GETTING BETTER, DARLING."
BUT SHE DIED AT ONE A.M.
ON THE DEATH CERTIFICATE, DR. PRITCHARD NOTED "PARALYSIS" AND "APOPLEXY" AS THE CAUSES OF MRS. TAYLOR'S DEMISE.
WHILE AT THE SAME TIME, ACTING ON HIS SUSPICIONS, DR. PATERSON WROTE THE DISTRICT REGISTRAR OF THE "MYSTERIOUS" DEATH.
BUT, FOR REASONS UNKNOWN, THE REGISTRAR'S OFFICE DISCARDED THE LETTER.

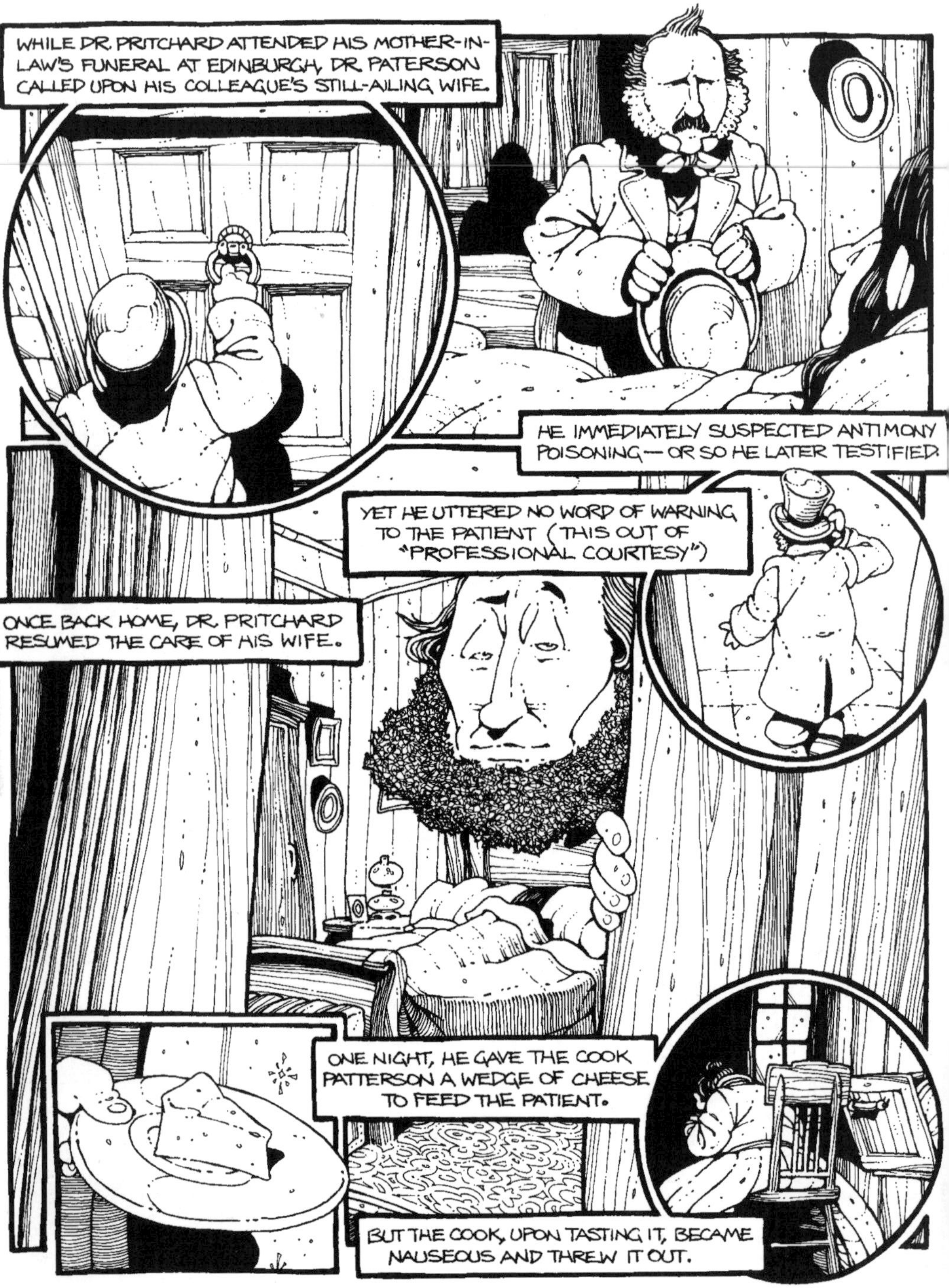
WHILE DR. PRITCHARD ATTENDED HIS MOTHER-IN-LAW'S FUNERAL AT EDINBURGH, DR. PATERSON CALLED UPON HIS COLLEAGUE'S STILL-AILING WIFE.
HE IMMEDIATELY SUSPECTED ANTIMONY POISONING — OR SO HE LATER TESTIFIED.
YET HE UTTERED NO WORD OF WARNING TO THE PATIENT (THIS OUT OF "PROFESSIONAL COURTESY")
ONCE BACK HOME, DR. PRITCHARD RESUMED THE CARE OF HIS WIFE.
ONE NIGHT, HE GAVE THE COOK PATTERSON A WEDGE OF CHEESE TO FEED THE PATIENT.
BUT THE COOK, UPON TASTING IT, BECAME NAUSEOUS AND THREW IT OUT.

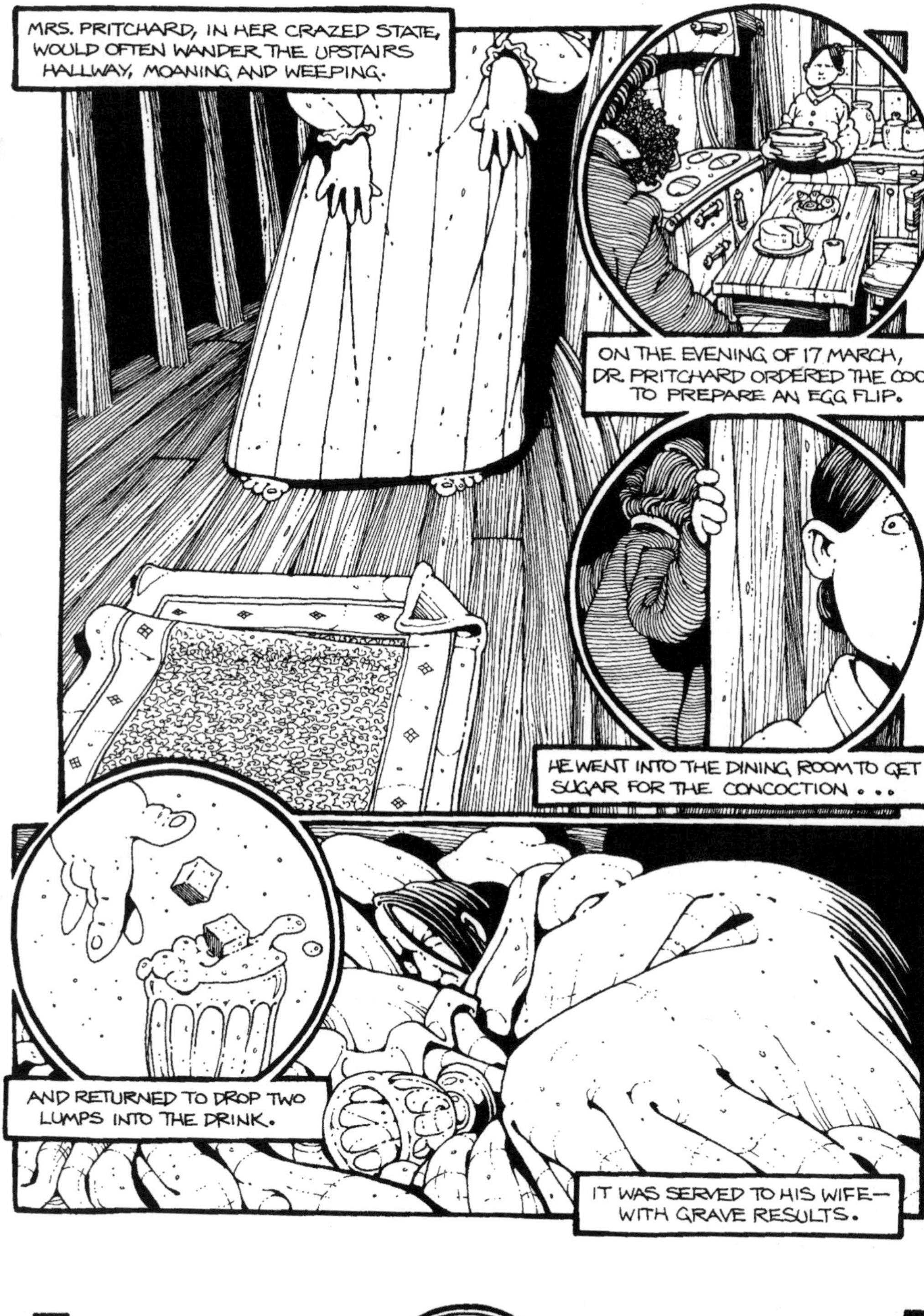
MRS. PRITCHARD, IN HER CRAZED STATE, WOULD OFTEN WANDER THE UPSTAIRS HALLWAY, MOANING AND WEEPING.
ON THE EVENING OF 17 MARCH, DR. PRITCHARD ORDERED THE COOK TO PREPARE AN EGG FLIP.
HE WENT INTO THE DINING ROOM TO GET SUGAR FOR THE CONCOCTION . . .
AND RETURNED TO DROP TWO LUMPS INTO THE DRINK.
IT WAS SERVED TO HIS WIFE– WITH GRAVE RESULTS.

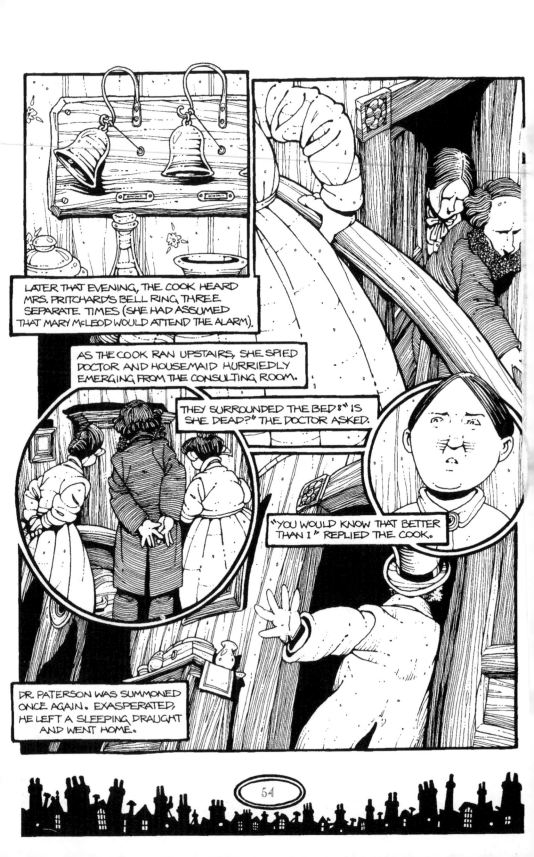

LATER THAT EVENING, THE COOK HEARD MRS. PRITCHARD'S BELL RING THREE SEPARATE TIMES (SHE HAD ASSUMED THAT MARY McLEOD WOULD ATTEND THE ALARM).

AS THE COOK RAN UPSTAIRS, SHE SPIED DOCTOR AND HOUSEMAID HURRIEDLY EMERGING FROM THE CONSULTING ROOM.

THEY SURROUNDED THE BED: "IS SHE DEAD?" THE DOCTOR ASKED.

"YOU WOULD KNOW THAT BETTER THAN I!" REPLIED THE COOK.

DR. PATERSON WAS SUMMONED ONCE AGAIN. EXASPERATED, HE LEFT A SLEEPING DRAUGHT AND WENT HOME.

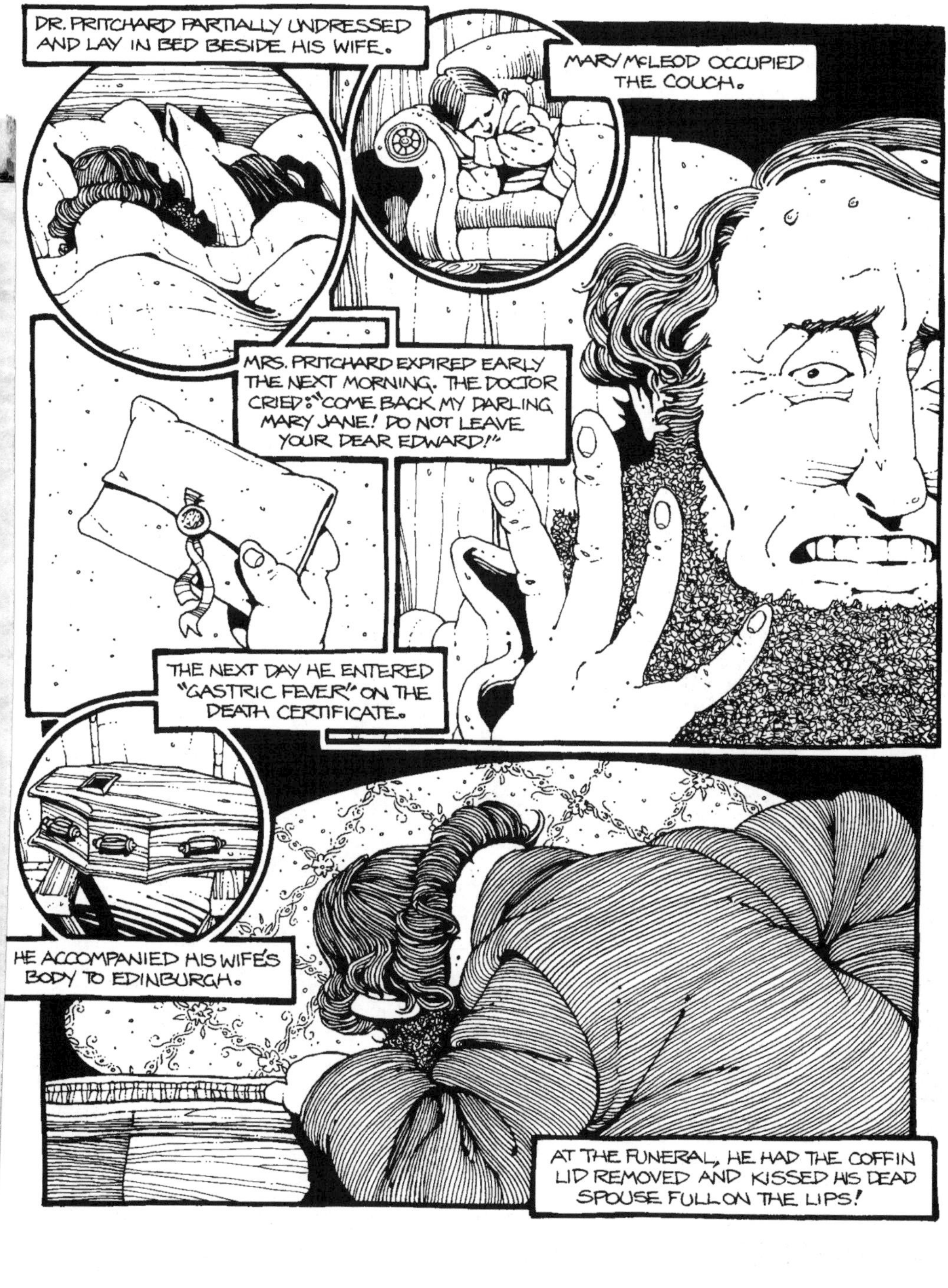
DR. PRITCHARD PARTIALLY UNDRESSED AND LAY IN BED BESIDE HIS WIFE.
MARY McLEOD OCCUPIED THE COUCH.
MRS. PRITCHARD EXPIRED EARLY THE NEXT MORNING. THE DOCTOR CRIED: "COME BACK MY DARLING MARY JANE! DO NOT LEAVE YOUR DEAR EDWARD!"
THE NEXT DAY HE ENTERED "GASTRIC FEVER" ON THE DEATH CERTIFICATE.
HE ACCOMPANIED HIS WIFE'S BODY TO EDINBURGH.
AT THE FUNERAL, HE HAD THE COFFIN LID REMOVED AND KISSED HIS DEAD SPOUSE FULL ON THE LIPS!

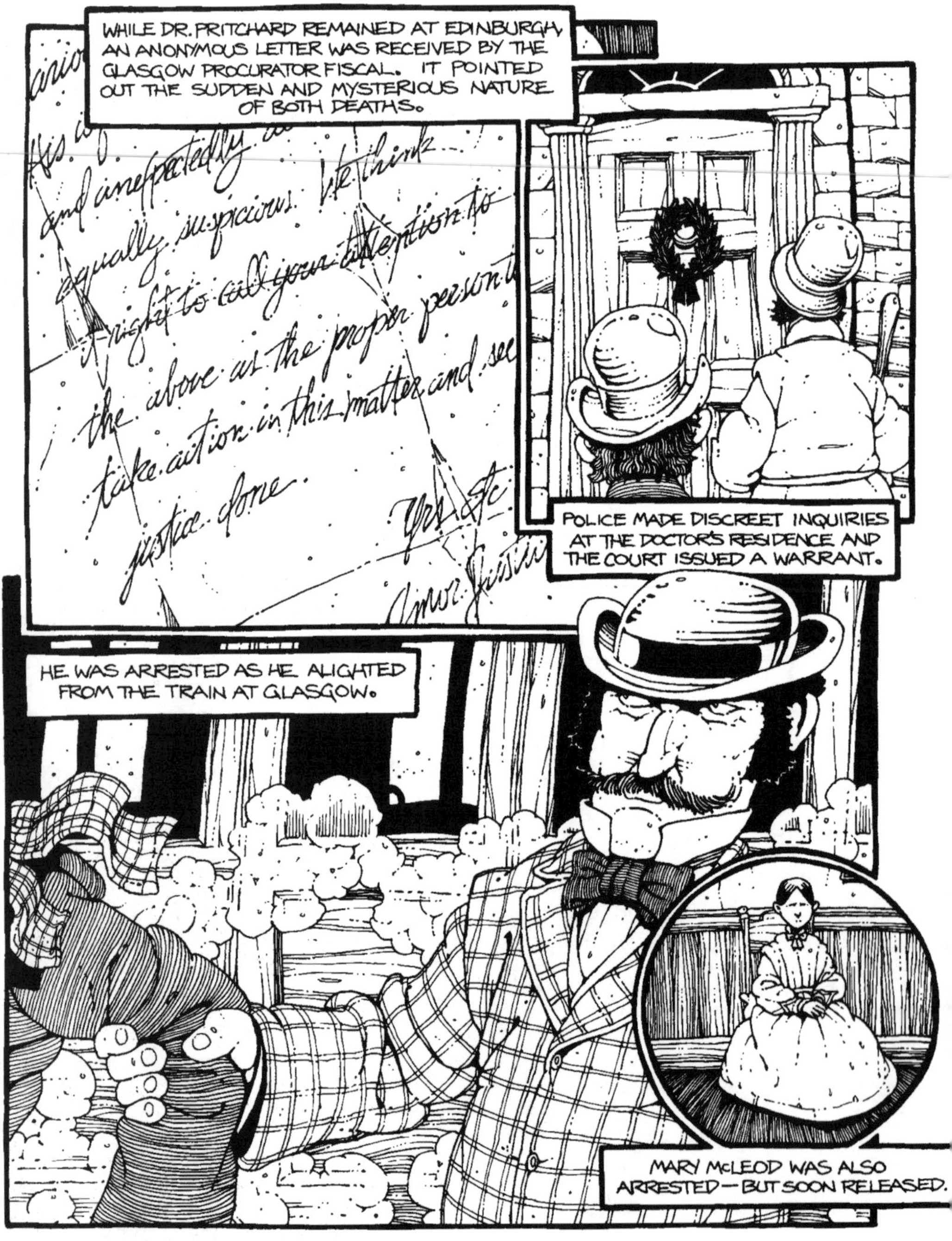
WHILE DR. PRITCHARD REMAINED AT EDINBURGH, AN ANONYMOUS LETTER WAS RECEIVED BY THE GLASGOW PROCURATOR FISCAL. IT POINTED OUT THE SUDDEN AND MYSTERIOUS NATURE OF BOTH DEATHS.
and unexpectedly
equally suspicious. We think
right to call your attention to
the above as the proper person
take action in this matter and see
justice done.
POLICE MADE DISCREET INQUIRIES AT THE DOCTOR'S RESIDENCE AND THE COURT ISSUED A WARRANT.
HE WAS ARRESTED AS HE ALIGHTED FROM THE TRAIN AT GLASGOW.
MARY McLEOD WAS ALSO ARRESTED—BUT SOON RELEASED.

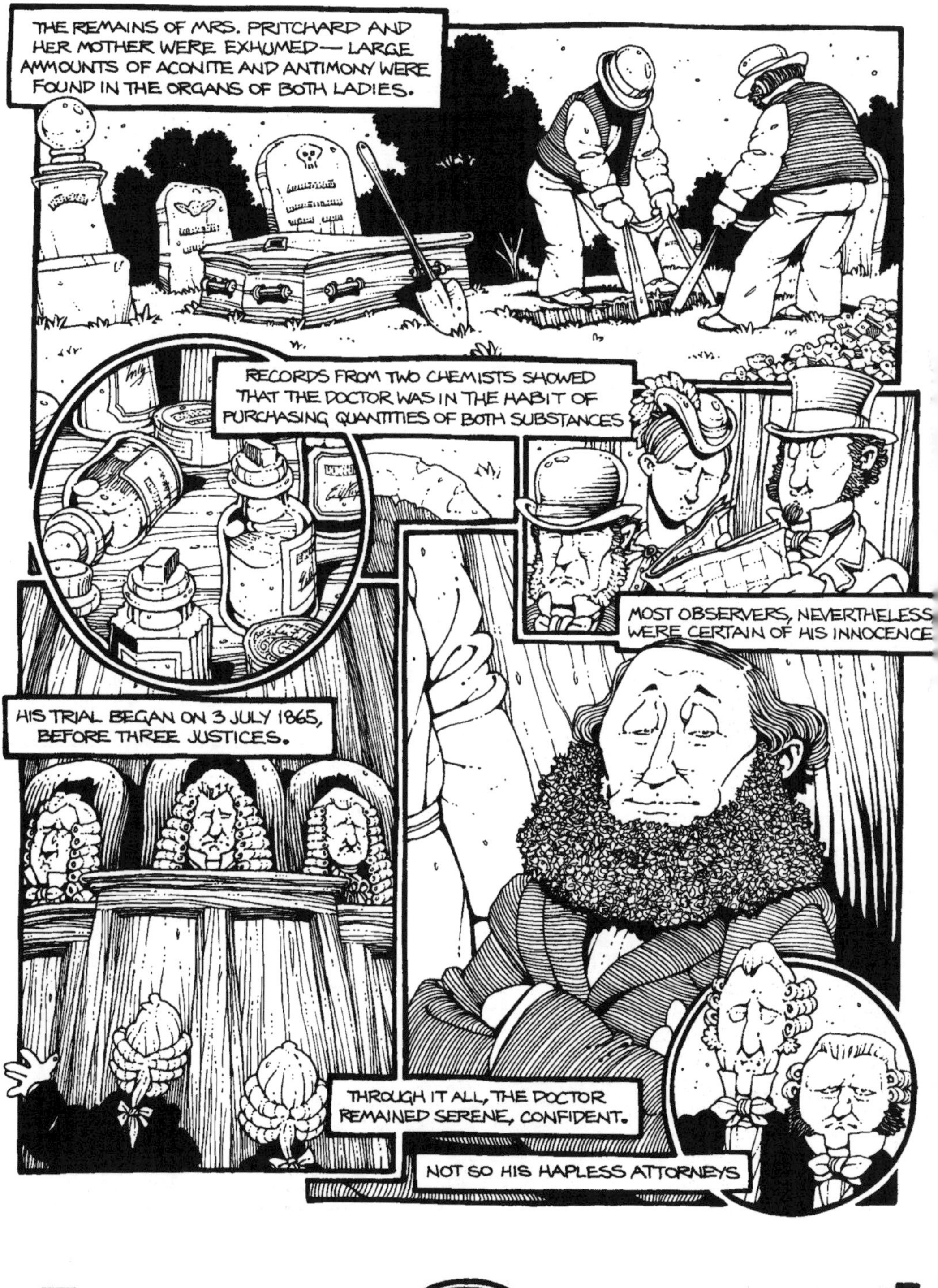
THE REMAINS OF MRS. PRITCHARD AND HER MOTHER WERE EXHUMED— LARGE AMMOUNTS OF ACONITE AND ANTIMONY WERE FOUND IN THE ORGANS OF BOTH LADIES.
RECORDS FROM TWO CHEMISTS SHOWED THAT THE DOCTOR WAS IN THE HABIT OF PURCHASING QUANTITIES OF BOTH SUBSTANCES
MOST OBSERVERS, NEVERTHELESS, WERE CERTAIN OF HIS INNOCENCE
HIS TRIAL BEGAN ON 3 JULY 1865, BEFORE THREE JUSTICES.
THROUGH IT ALL, THE DOCTOR REMAINED SERENE, CONFIDENT.
NOT SO HIS HAPLESS ATTORNEYS

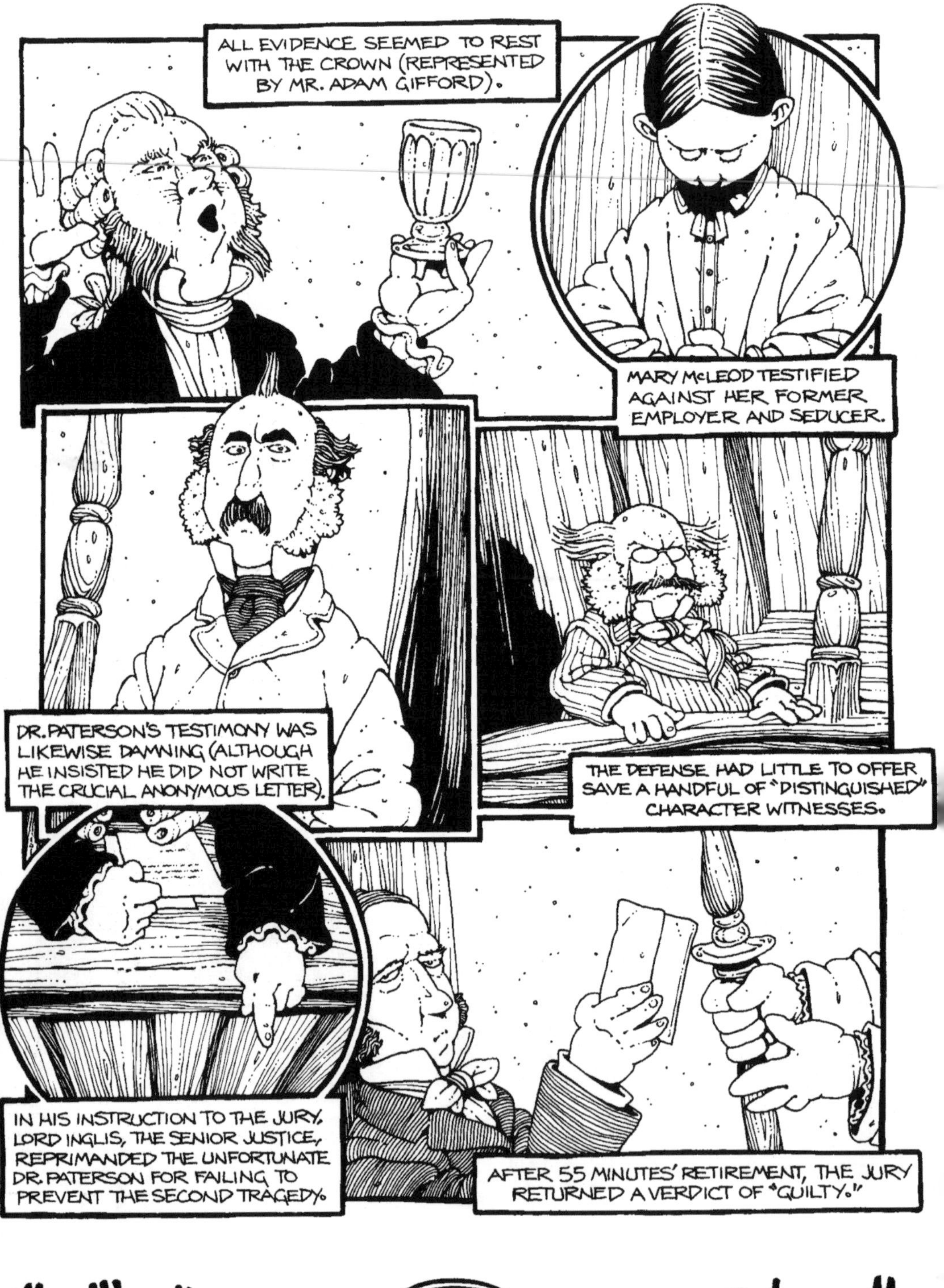
ALL EVIDENCE SEEMED TO REST WITH THE CROWN (REPRESENTED BY MR. ADAM GIFFORD).
MARY McLEOD TESTIFIED AGAINST HER FORMER EMPLOYER AND SEDUCER.
DR. PATERSON'S TESTIMONY WAS LIKEWISE DAMNING (ALTHOUGH HE INSISTED HE DID NOT WRITE THE CRUCIAL ANONYMOUS LETTER).
THE DEFENSE HAD LITTLE TO OFFER SAVE A HANDFUL OF "DISTINGUISHED" CHARACTER WITNESSES.
IN HIS INSTRUCTION TO THE JURY, LORD INGLIS, THE SENIOR JUSTICE, REPRIMANDED THE UNFORTUNATE DR. PATERSON FOR FAILING TO PREVENT THE SECOND TRAGEDY.
AFTER 55 MINUTES' RETIREMENT, THE JURY RETURNED A VERDICT OF "GUILTY."

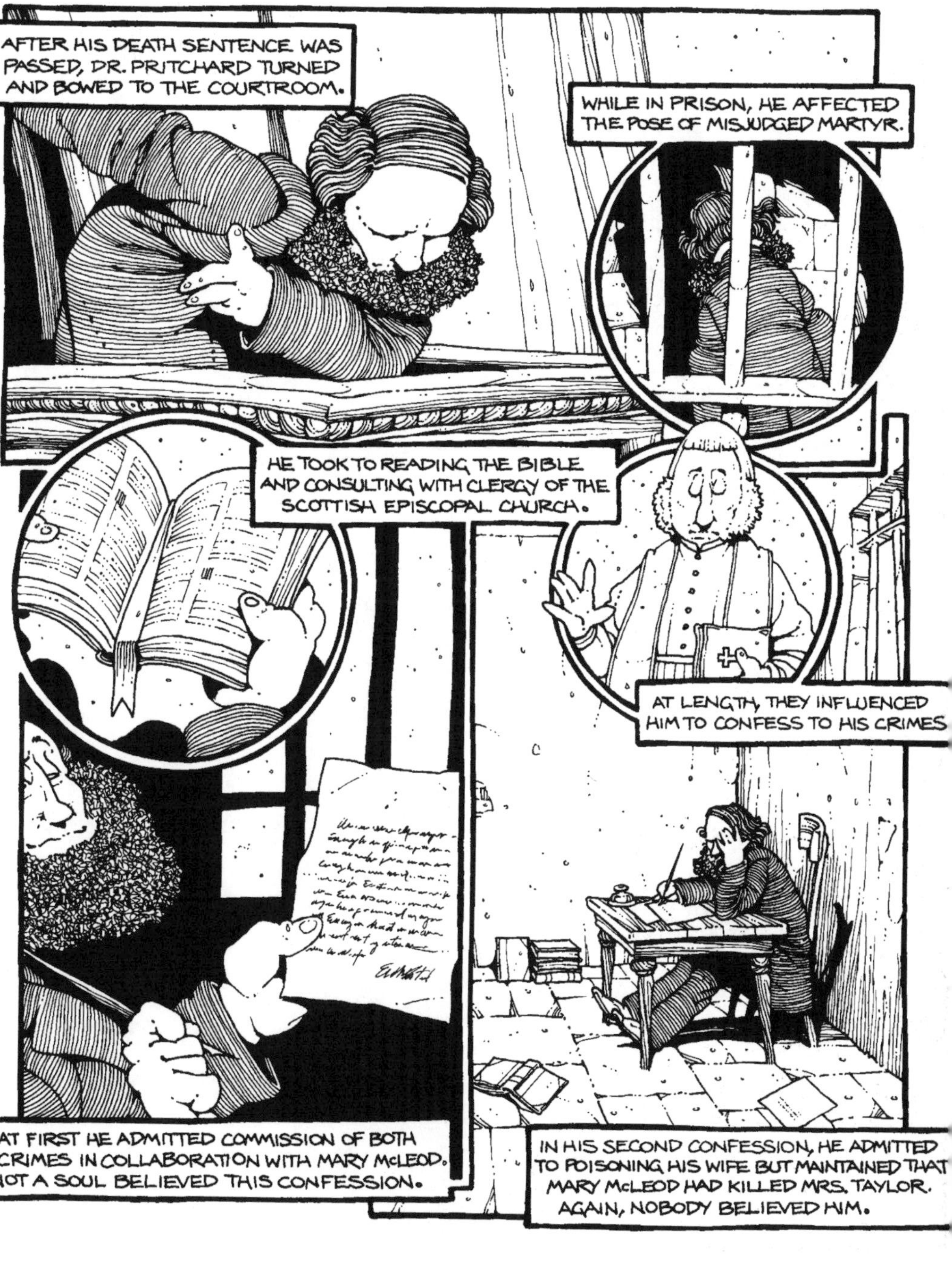

AFTER HIS DEATH SENTENCE WAS PASSED, DR. PRITCHARD TURNED AND BOWED TO THE COURTROOM.
WHILE IN PRISON, HE AFFECTED THE POSE OF MISJUDGED MARTYR.
HE TOOK TO READING THE BIBLE AND CONSULTING WITH CLERGY OF THE SCOTTISH EPISCOPAL CHURCH.
AT LENGTH, THEY INFLUENCED HIM TO CONFESS TO HIS CRIMES
AT FIRST HE ADMITTED COMMISSION OF BOTH CRIMES IN COLLABORATION WITH MARY McLEOD. NOT A SOUL BELIEVED THIS CONFESSION.
IN HIS SECOND CONFESSION, HE ADMITTED TO POISONING HIS WIFE BUT MAINTAINED THAT MARY McLEOD HAD KILLED MRS. TAYLOR. AGAIN, NOBODY BELIEVED HIM.

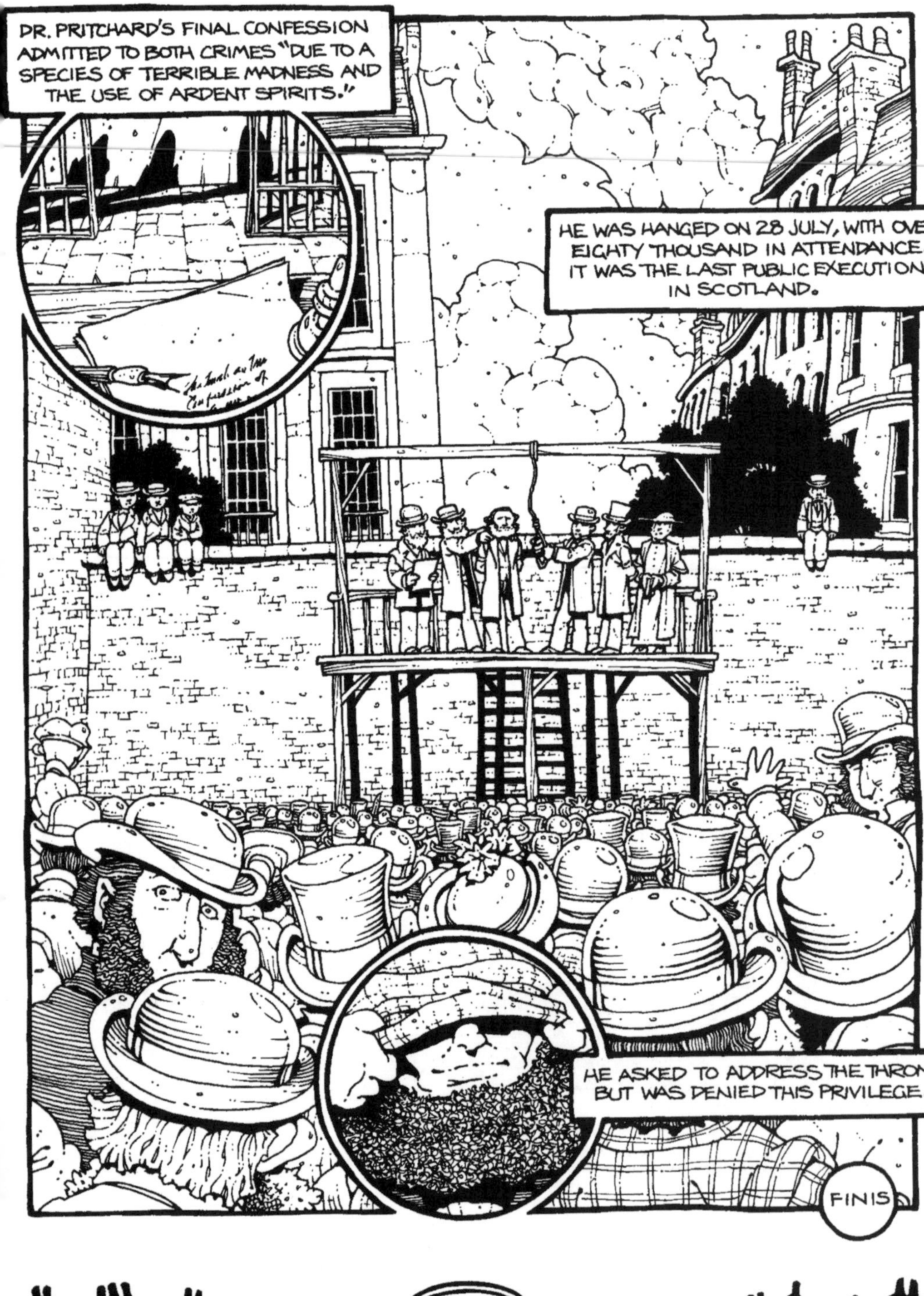
DR. PRITCHARD'S FINAL CONFESSION ADMITTED TO BOTH CRIMES "DUE TO A SPECIES OF TERRIBLE MADNESS AND THE USE OF ARDENT SPIRITS."
HE WAS HANGED ON 28 JULY, WITH OVER EIGHTY THOUSAND IN ATTENDANCE. IT WAS THE LAST PUBLIC EXECUTION IN SCOTLAND.
HE ASKED TO ADDRESS THE THRONG BUT WAS DENIED THIS PRIVILEGE.
FINIS

# THE ABOMINABLE
# MRS. PEARCEY

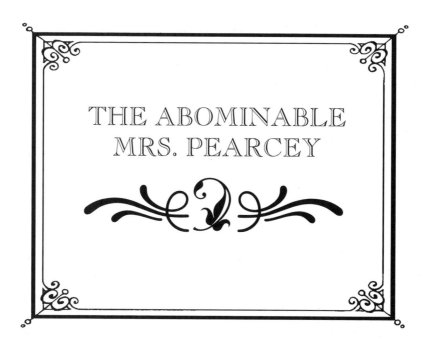

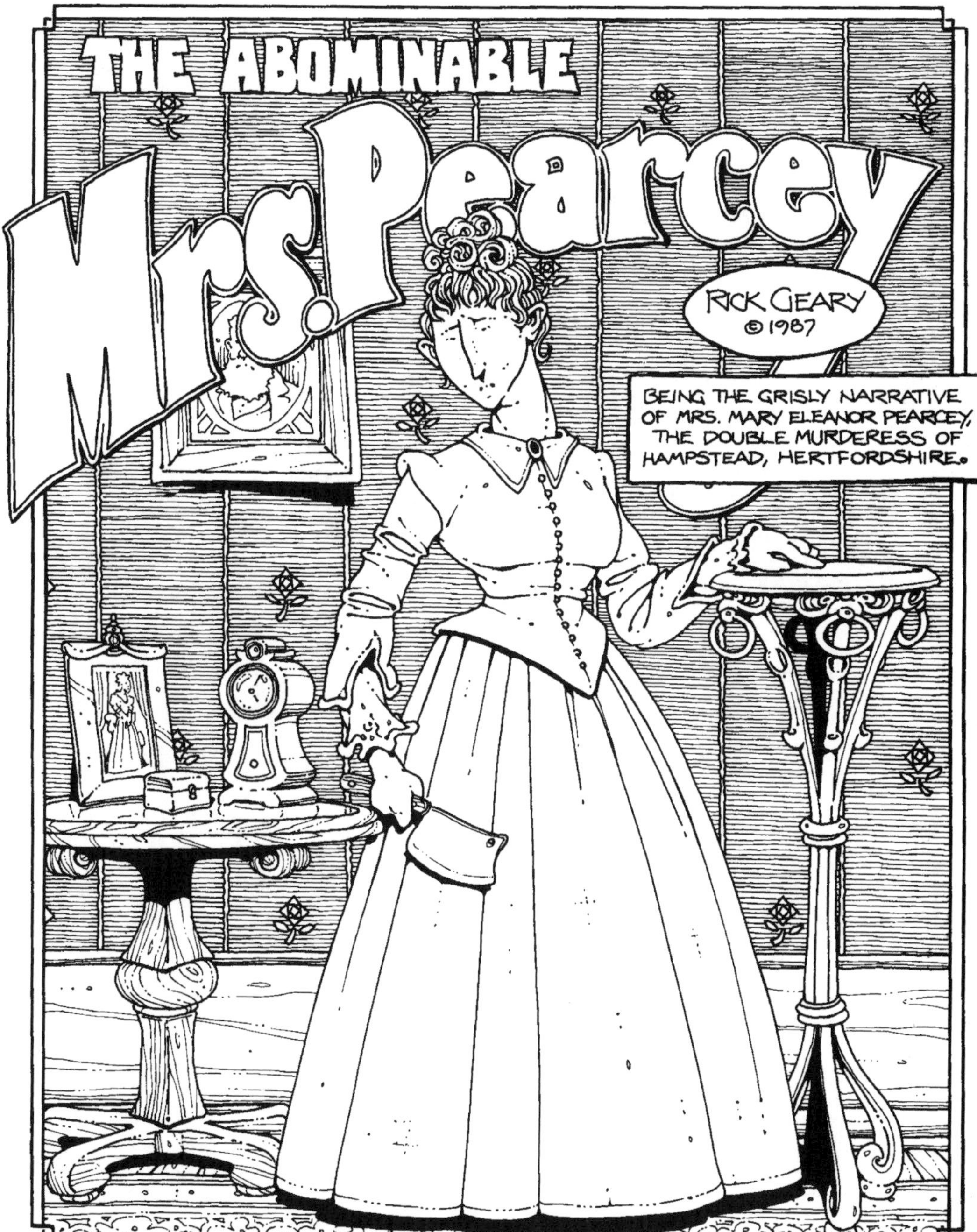
THE ABOMINABLE
Mrs. Pearcey
RICK GEARY
©1987
BEING THE GRISLY NARRATIVE OF MRS. MARY ELEANOR PEARCEY, THE DOUBLE MURDERESS OF HAMPSTEAD, HERTFORDSHIRE.

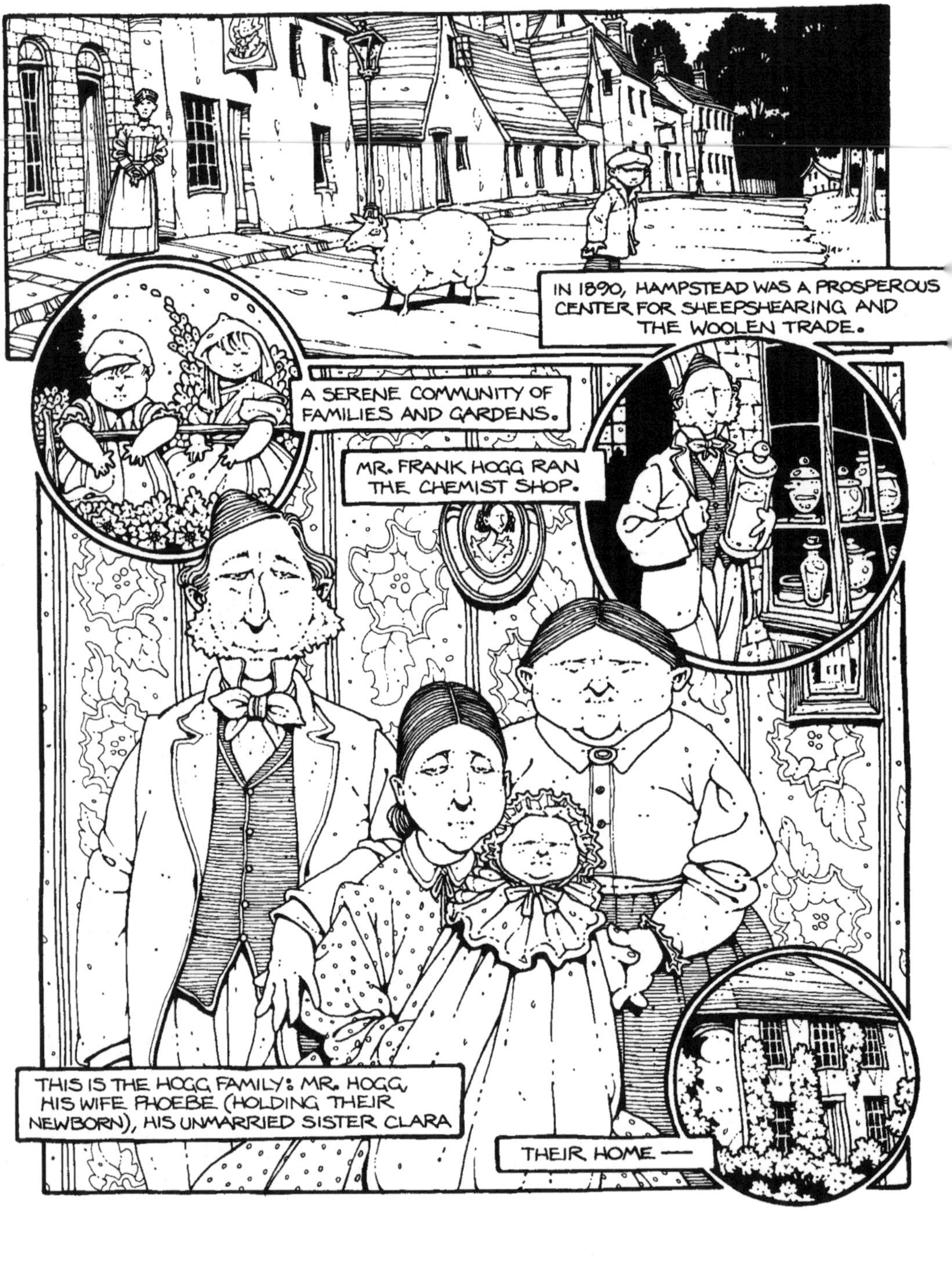
IN 1890, HAMPSTEAD WAS A PROSPEROUS CENTER FOR SHEEPSHEARING AND THE WOOLEN TRADE.
A SERENE COMMUNITY OF FAMILIES AND GARDENS.
MR. FRANK HOGG RAN THE CHEMIST SHOP.
THIS IS THE HOGG FAMILY: MR. HOGG, HIS WIFE PHOEBE (HOLDING THEIR NEWBORN), HIS UNMARRIED SISTER CLARA
THEIR HOME —

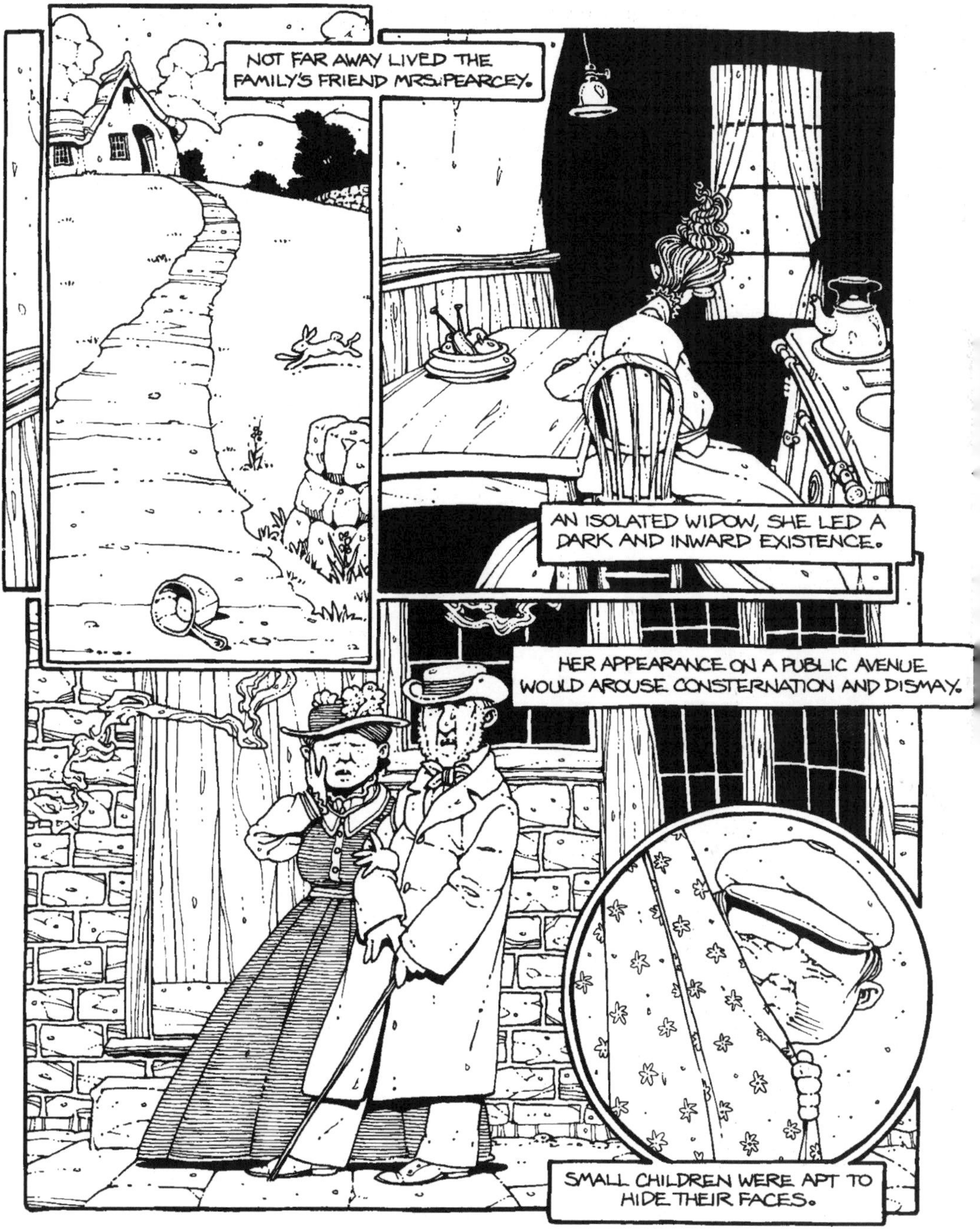
NOT FAR AWAY LIVED THE FAMILY'S FRIEND MRS. PEARCEY.
AN ISOLATED WIDOW, SHE LED A DARK AND INWARD EXISTENCE.
HER APPEARANCE ON A PUBLIC AVENUE WOULD AROUSE CONSTERNATION AND DISMAY.
SMALL CHILDREN WERE APT TO HIDE THEIR FACES.

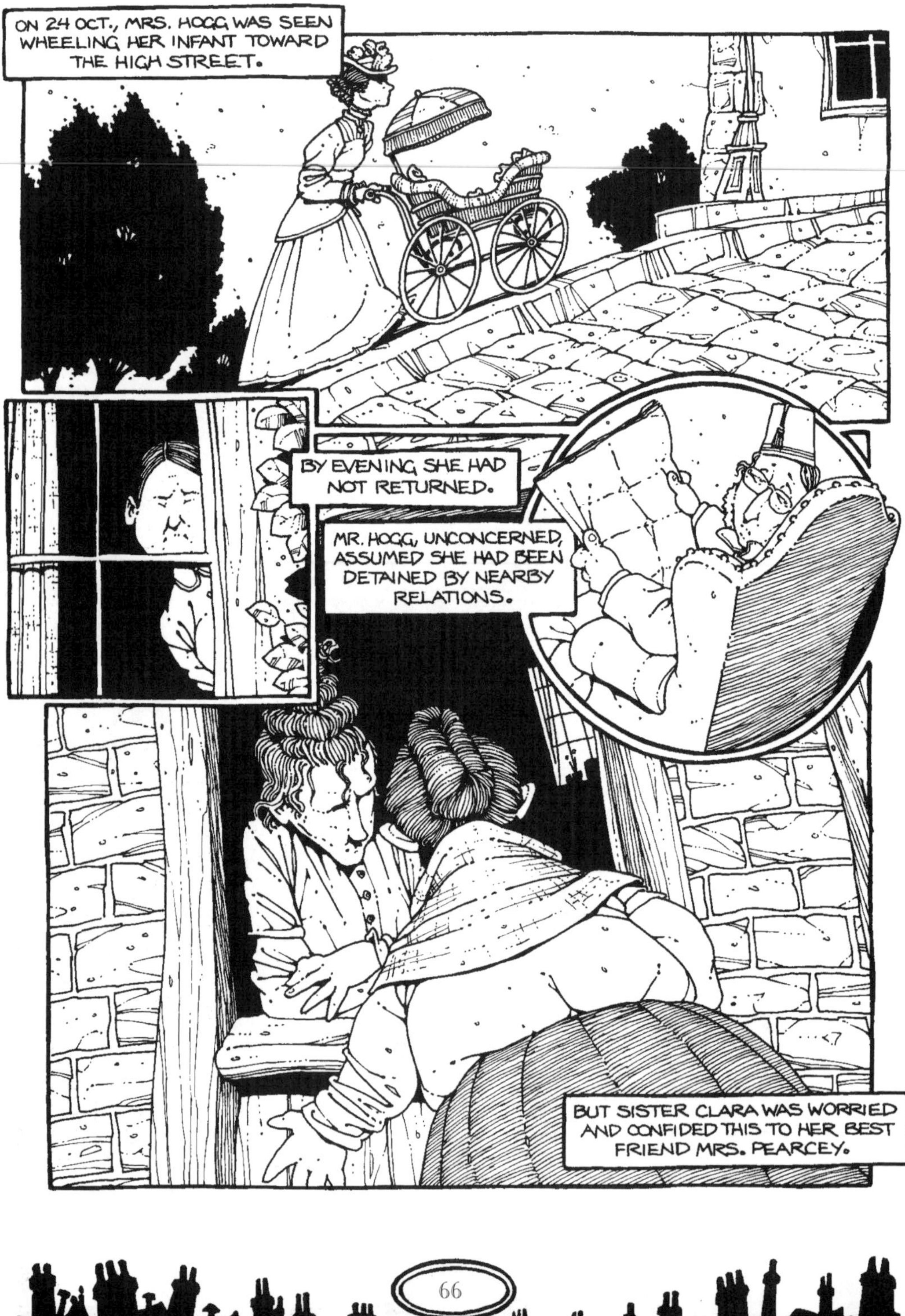
ON 24 OCT., MRS. HOGG WAS SEEN WHEELING HER INFANT TOWARD THE HIGH STREET.
BY EVENING SHE HAD NOT RETURNED.
MR. HOGG, UNCONCERNED, ASSUMED SHE HAD BEEN DETAINED BY NEARBY RELATIONS.
BUT SISTER CLARA WAS WORRIED AND CONFIDED THIS TO HER BEST FRIEND MRS. PEARCEY.

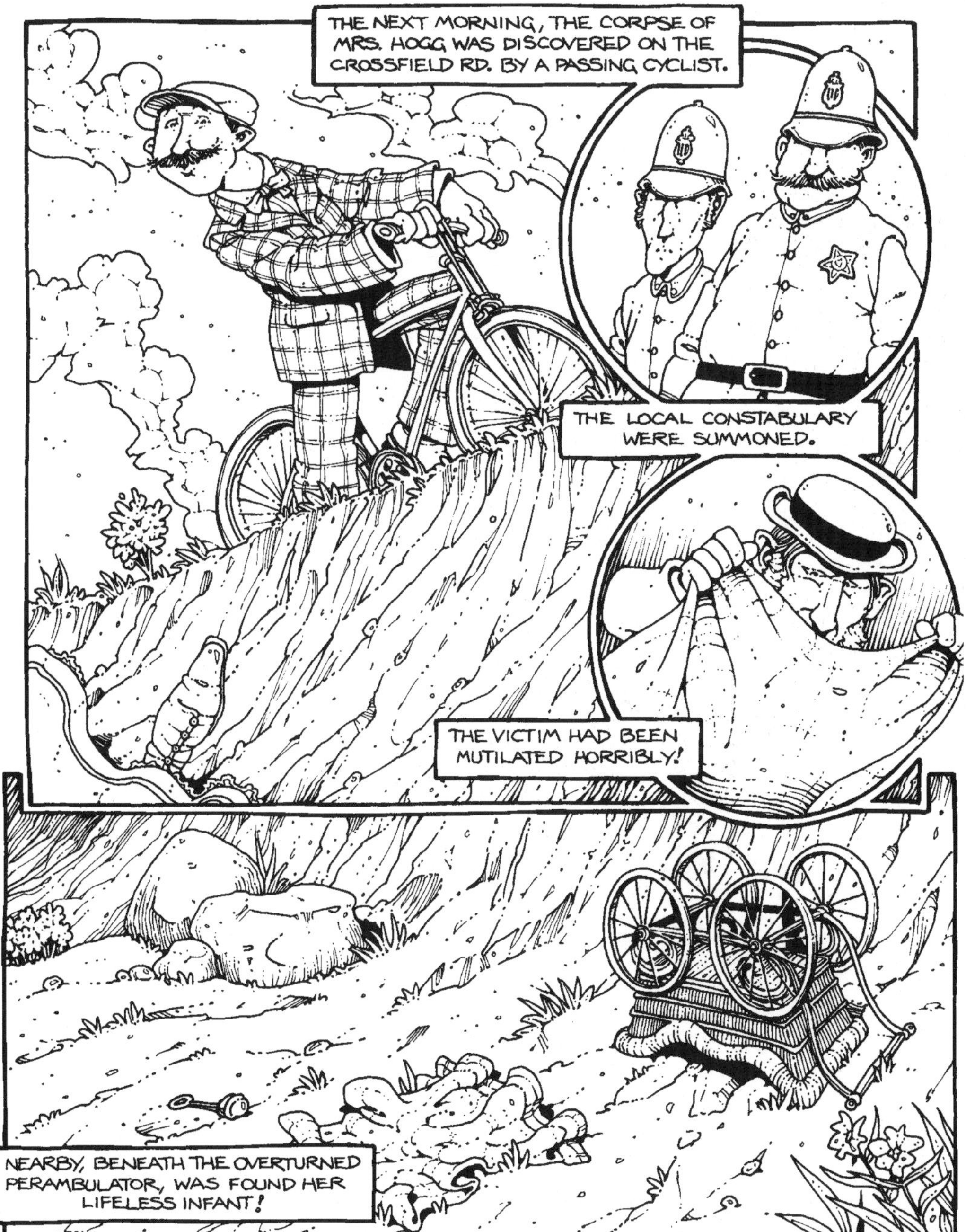
THE NEXT MORNING, THE CORPSE OF MRS. HOGG WAS DISCOVERED ON THE CROSSFIELD RD. BY A PASSING CYCLIST.
THE LOCAL CONSTABULARY WERE SUMMONED.
THE VICTIM HAD BEEN MUTILATED HORRIBLY!
NEARBY, BENEATH THE OVERTURNED PERAMBULATOR, WAS FOUND HER LIFELESS INFANT!

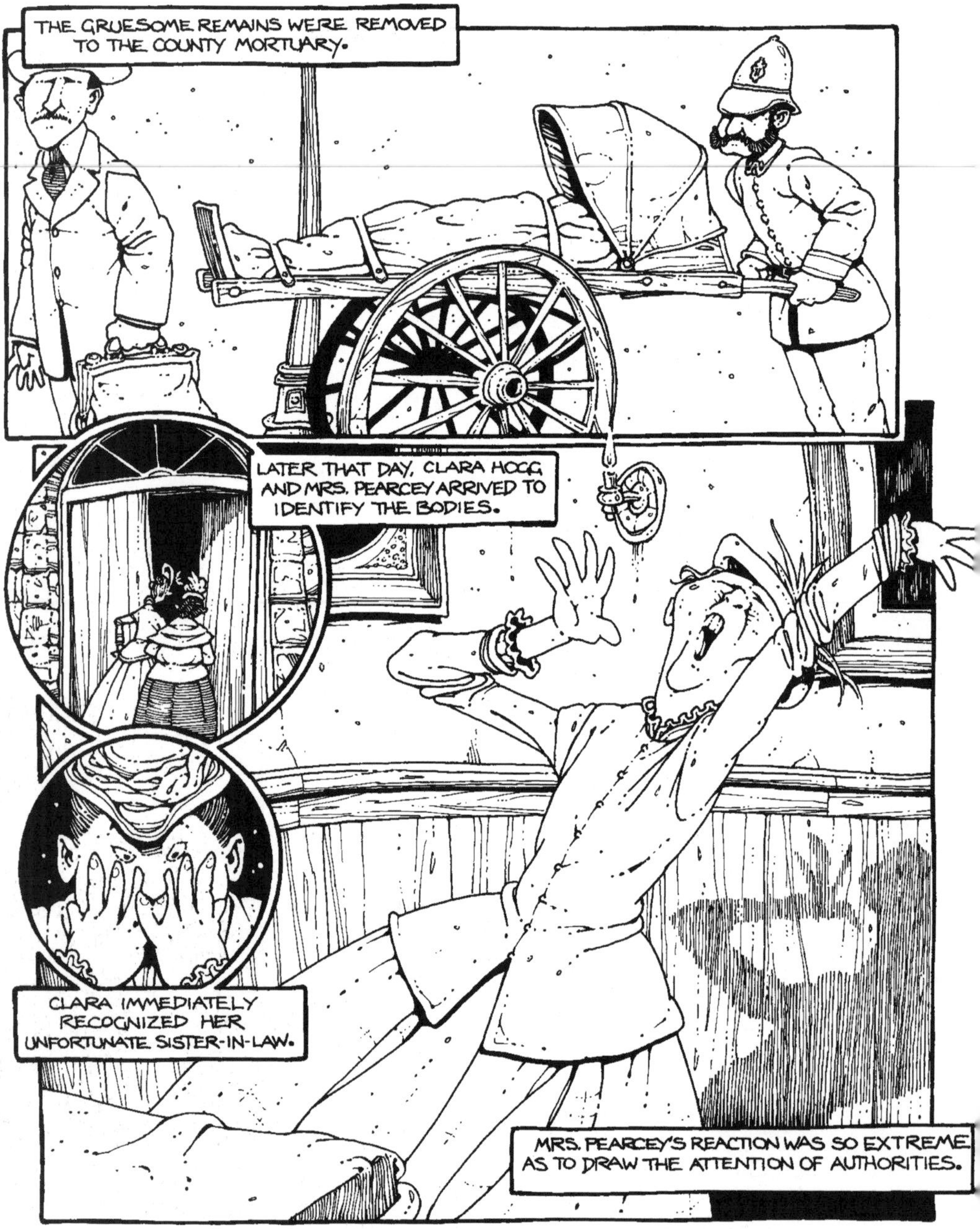
THE GRUESOME REMAINS WERE REMOVED TO THE COUNTY MORTUARY.
LATER THAT DAY, CLARA HOGG AND MRS. PEARCEY ARRIVED TO IDENTIFY THE BODIES.
CLARA IMMEDIATELY RECOGNIZED HER UNFORTUNATE SISTER-IN-LAW.
MRS. PEARCEY'S REACTION WAS SO EXTREME AS TO DRAW THE ATTENTION OF AUTHORITIES.

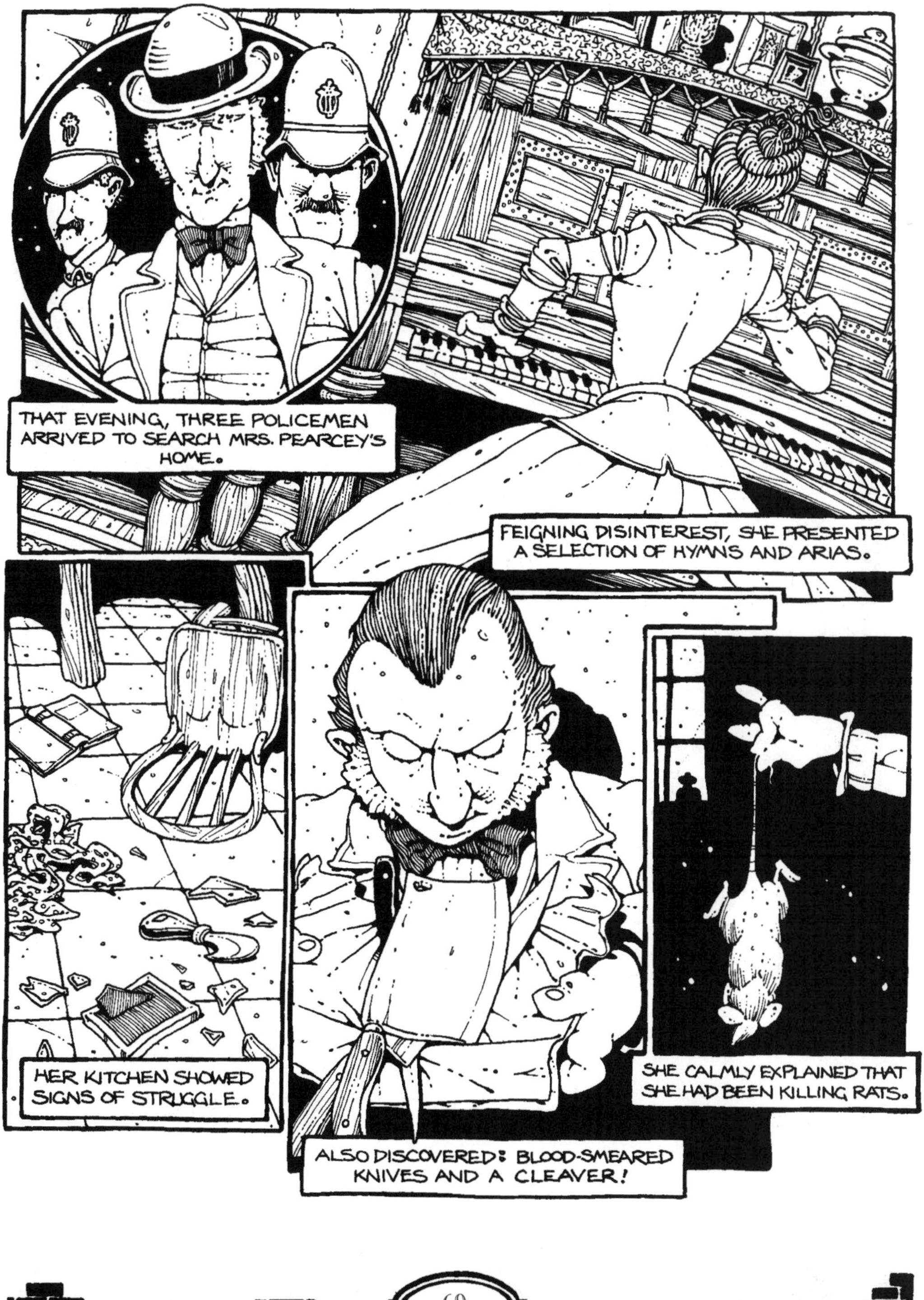
THAT EVENING, THREE POLICEMEN ARRIVED TO SEARCH MRS. PEARCEY'S HOME.
FEIGNING DISINTEREST, SHE PRESENTED A SELECTION OF HYMNS AND ARIAS.
HER KITCHEN SHOWED SIGNS OF STRUGGLE.
ALSO DISCOVERED: BLOOD-SMEARED KNIVES AND A CLEAVER!
SHE CALMLY EXPLAINED THAT SHE HAD BEEN KILLING RATS.

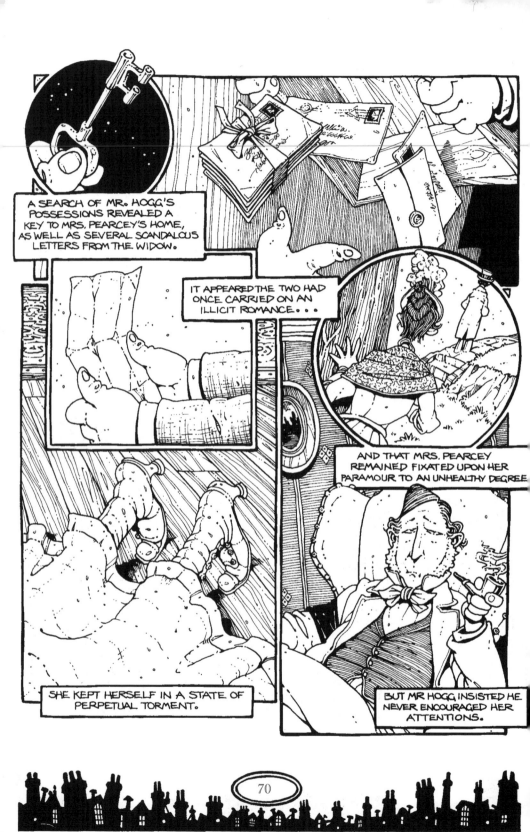

A SEARCH OF MR. HOGG'S POSSESSIONS REVEALED A KEY TO MRS. PEARCEY'S HOME, AS WELL AS SEVERAL SCANDALOUS LETTERS FROM THE WIDOW.

IT APPEARED THE TWO HAD ONCE CARRIED ON AN ILLICIT ROMANCE . . .

AND THAT MRS. PEARCEY REMAINED FIXATED UPON HER PARAMOUR TO AN UNHEALTHY DEGREE.

SHE KEPT HERSELF IN A STATE OF PERPETUAL TORMENT.

BUT MR. HOGG INSISTED HE NEVER ENCOURAGED HER ATTENTIONS.

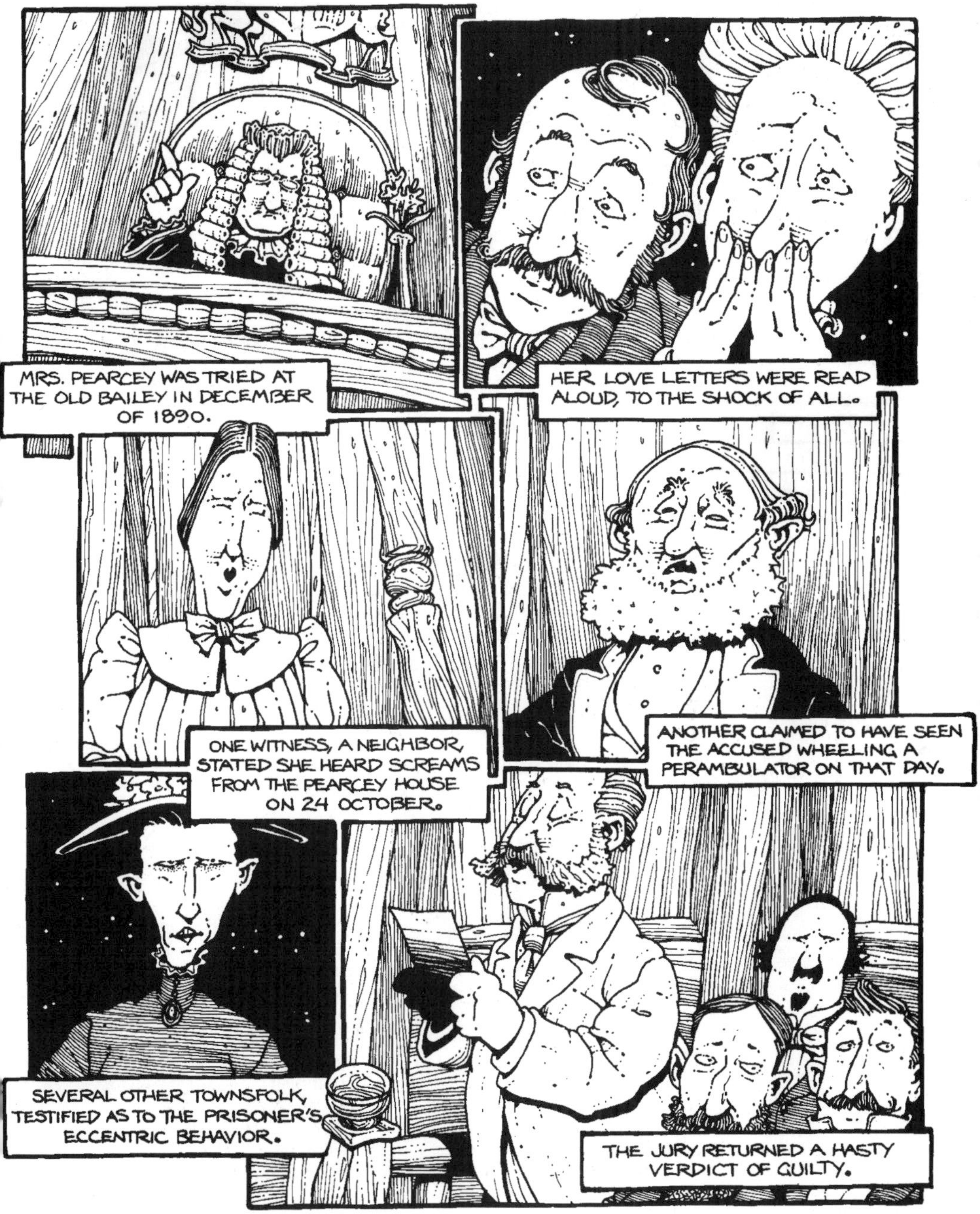
MRS. PEARCEY WAS TRIED AT THE OLD BAILEY IN DECEMBER OF 1890.
HER LOVE LETTERS WERE READ ALOUD, TO THE SHOCK OF ALL.
ONE WITNESS, A NEIGHBOR, STATED SHE HEARD SCREAMS FROM THE PEARCEY HOUSE ON 24 OCTOBER.
ANOTHER CLAIMED TO HAVE SEEN THE ACCUSED WHEELING A PERAMBULATOR ON THAT DAY.
SEVERAL OTHER TOWNSFOLK TESTIFIED AS TO THE PRISONER'S ECCENTRIC BEHAVIOR.
THE JURY RETURNED A HASTY VERDICT OF GUILTY.

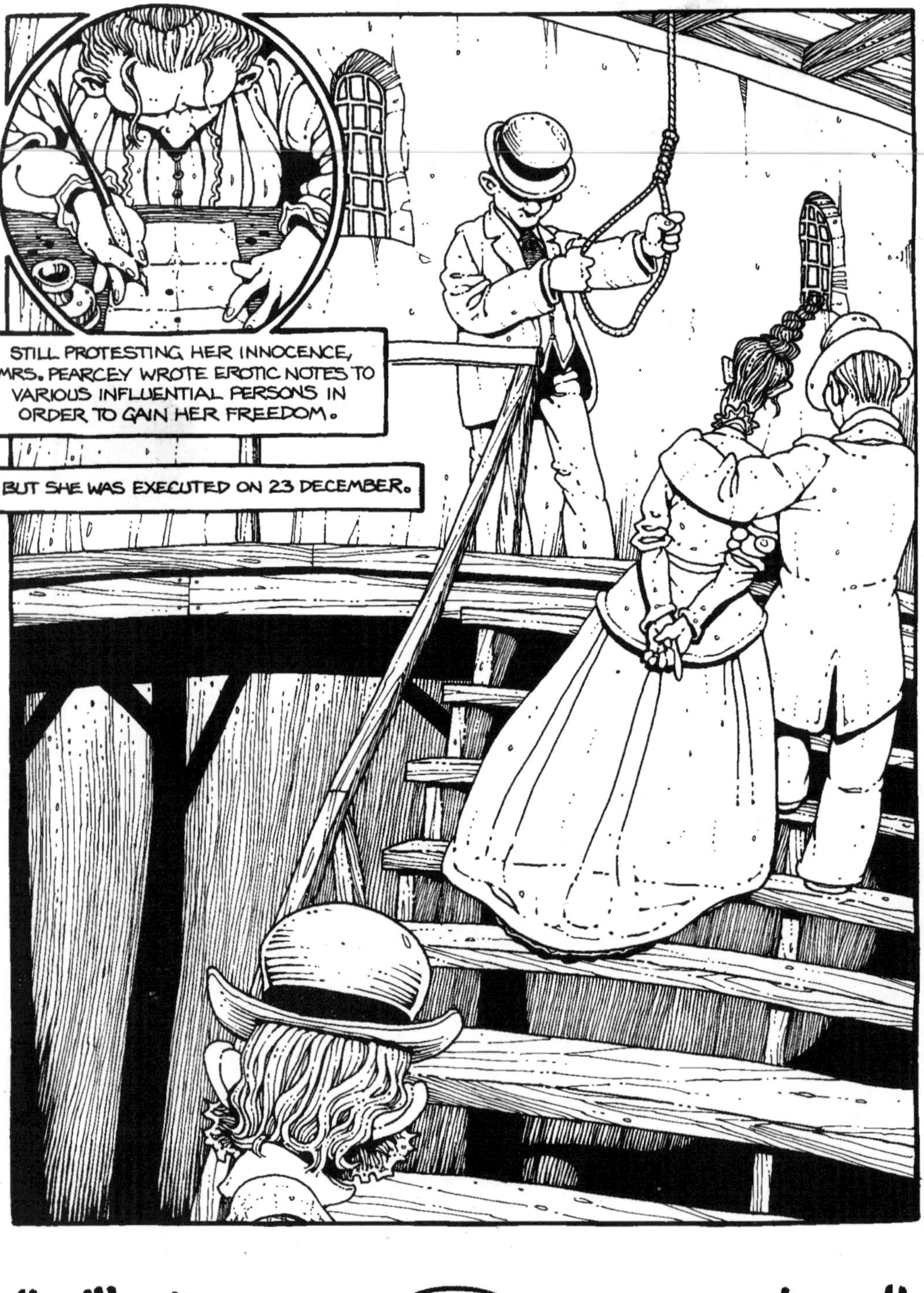
STILL PROTESTING HER INNOCENCE, MRS. PEARCEY WROTE EROTIC NOTES TO VARIOUS INFLUENTIAL PERSONS IN ORDER TO GAIN HER FREEDOM.
BUT SHE WAS EXECUTED ON 23 DECEMBER.